"*Dynamic Play and Creative Movement* is timely, enlivening, and creative. This book will show teachers, parents, school administrators, school boards, and those who teach teachers how a classroom can come alive—even as deeper learning becomes accessible. This is indeed exciting."

Beate Becker, *MA, MS, BC-DMT, PA,*
CMA, SEP, LMHC

"I believe this book to be on the leading edge of a growing field—of dance or movement therapy—which can serve important needs for postsecondary faculty teaching education and special education courses. Elementary school teachers, social workers, paraprofessionals, clinicians, and special education teachers looking to add these action-oriented concepts and methods into their curricula and classrooms would benefit, as well as parents hoping to stimulate maximum brain development in their children."

Mary C. Starke, *professor of Clinical Psychology,*
Ramapo College of New Jersey

"Judith Peck beautifully brings to life the inherent qualities in all children: energy, imagination, movement and creativity. The mind is never independent of the physical body. In this book Judith demonstrates how movement and creative expression are essential for learning and brain development."

Jean Seibel, *MA, LCAT, BC-DMT, visiting professor*
Pratt Institute Graduate Dance Therapy Program

"Dancers and footballers have to move to think. They think by moving. And so do children. In this much needed antidote to sedentary education, Judith Peck guides us skillfully through the research behind this claim, and the many benefits which movement bestows on children's intellectual as well as physical development. So, teachers, get moving!"

Guy Claxton, *author of* Intelligence in the Flesh

Dynamic Play and Creative Movement

Dynamic Play and Creative Movement offers effective methods to supplement elementary education for young children using dance, movement, and play.

Imagination, physical energy, and the need for self-expression are childhood qualities recognized by parents but not sufficiently valued to be applied to formal education. Yet when valued as natural endowments, they might intelligently be used to increase a child's perceptive abilities and self-confidence, essential to learning. These three qualities combine in *dynamic play*, a term devised by the author to describe an approach to learning. Through physical participation, children deal with concepts, ideas, and emotions while they reach out to touch a vast world of people, animals, nature, and activities. The chapters provide for improvisations in music, visual art, drama and stories in addition to topics related to the changing seasons, sports, school subjects, travel, games, and many other elements of the natural and man-made world. Research about the correlation of movement to brain activity is included to support the thesis that creative movement is an effective adjunct to learning.

Therapists, counselors, and preschool and elementary school teachers will find this easily adaptable material valuable in fostering perception, insight, and cognitive understanding in children.

Dr. Judith Peck is a sculptor, professor emerita of art, and author of several books on art technique, movement, and parenting, as well as two novels and award-winning children's picture books.

Dynamic Play and Creative Movement

Powering Body and Brain

Judith Peck, Ed.D.

Routledge
Taylor & Francis Group

NEW YORK AND LONDON

Cover image: Getty Image

First published 2023
by Routledge
605 Third Avenue, New York, NY 10158

and by Routledge
4 Park Square, Milton Park, Abingdon, Oxon,
OX14 4RN

*Routledge is an imprint of the Taylor & Francis Group,
an informa business*

Library of Congress Cataloging-in-Publication Data
Names: Peck, Judith, author.
Title: Dynamic play and creative movement : powering
    body and brain / by Judith Peck.
Description: New York, NY : Routledge, [2023] |
    Includes bibliographical references and index.
Identifiers: LCCN 2022020731 (print) | LCCN 2022020732
    (ebook) | ISBN 9781032184982 (hardback) | ISBN
    9781032184944 (paperback) | ISBN 9781003254812 (ebook)
Subjects: LCSH: Movement education—Study and teaching
    (Elementary) | Learning—Physiological aspects. | Art in
    education. | Dance in education.
Classification: LCC GV452 .P43 2023 (print) | LCC GV452
    (ebook) | DDC 372.86/8044—dc23/eng/20220810
LC record available at https://lccn.loc.gov/2022020731
LC ebook record available at https://lccn.loc.gov/2022020732

ISBN: 978-1-032-18498-2 (hbk)
ISBN: 978-1-032-18494-4 (pbk)
ISBN: 978-1-003-25481-2 (ebk)

DOI: 10.4324/9781003254812

Typeset in NewBaskerville
by Apex CoVantage, LLC

Judith Peck holds a doctoral degree from New York University and two master's degrees from Teachers College, Columbia University. She is a professional member of the American Art Therapy Association, the Authors Guild, and the Sculptors Guild. Dr. Peck is the author of several books in the area of arts technique and education. She is Professor Emerita of Art at Ramapo College of New Jersey, Mahwah, New Jersey; her sculpture is included in 80 public and private collections.

https://jpecksculpture.com
https://iapbooks.com
JudithPeck@optonline.net

Other Books by Judith Peck

Leap to the Sun: Learning through Dynamic Play

Sculpture as Experience: Working with Clay, Wire, Wax, Plaster and Found Objects

Sculpture as Experience 2nd Expanded Edition

Smart Starts in the Arts: Fostering Intelligence, Creativity and Serenity in the Early Years

Art Activities for Mind and Imagination

Artistic Crafts: Inventive Creations from Cast-offs

Seeing in the Dark: Arielle's Story, novel

Naked Under the Lights, novel

Runaway Piggy Bank, children's picture book

The Bright Blue Button and the Button-Hole, children's picture book

Credit line: *Courtesy of Alice Teirstein*

This book is dedicated to the children who inspired it.

To yours, who will use it in inventive ways.

To mine, whose achievements and humanity continue to inspire —Sarah, Jamie, Joel, and Sabrina.

Contents

Foreword

Over my desk come many requests for review and consideration of materials for use in our public school system. With the numerous pressures and demands made on boards of education today, I must admit that it is left with little time to devote to the reading of educational materials.

When Judith Peck sent her book to me for review, I perused it rather hurriedly and then put it aside for future reading if and when time permitted. Somehow, the photographs and the contents generally captured my interest and haunted me so that I had to pull it out of the pile of manuscripts and reread it.

On second and more careful reading, I was convinced that every child in the school system should be exposed to Judith Peck's unique approach to the teaching of the arts. An imaginative teacher, and even one with less imagination, would find the contents stimulating, and in turn, the children would be equally stimulated.

Unfortunately, we do not have sufficient texts that possess this quality of appeal and value for the urban child. As Superintendent Helene Lloyd, an expert in curriculum evaluation, states, "The suggestions and excellent photographs would motivate teachers and group leaders to develop expressive movements with children. This is an area not emphasized sufficiently in all schools over the country."

I support wholeheartedly Mrs. Lloyd's appraisal and trust that teachers all over the country will be given the opportunity to use this superb book.

Rose Shapiro
(Former President, New York City Board of Education)

Preface

I wrote my first book on the subject, *Leap to the Sun: Learning through Dynamic Play*, 43 years ago when I became aware of a fascinating situation. Of approximately a hundred young children in my creative movement classes, very nearly all were fully engaged physically, mentally, and creatively: eagerly moving their bodies, focused, and full of inventive ideas. I was on to something. Using their physical energy to express ideas that interested them tapped into resources they had used all along to understand things. How quickly they wrapped their heads around an idea. How spontaneously they directed their bodies into interpretations of that idea. How integrated became the brain, the body, the activity, and the learning.

At the time, I had made no studies of brain–movement connections and didn't think along those lines. But seeing the responsiveness to these ideas propelled by movement, I formulated a reason behind my observations: I was seeing an ebullient mind–body integration as the children searched their visual experience to relate to the topic, instinctively attached their feelings to it, and then moved their bodies to bring the images to life.

The children within my two sets of classes were of late preschool and early grade-school age. Because they were young and fully engaged, I reasoned that this way of learning was natural to them. As if they had been using it all along, possibly from birth. I called this legacy "natural endowments" and recognized these to be (1) vast physical energy, (2) a vivid imagination, and (3) a fierce need for self-expression. The projects I was leading them in, which became the content of that earlier book, tapped into all three. This was fertile grounds for learning. Physical energy put in use to express imaginative ideas activated cognitive connection-making. And one other observation: As you look at the photographs of children scattered through these pages, it is hard not to notice the joyfulness in their engagement.

Educators recognized that *Leap to the Sun* offered a uniquely viable way to connect the natural abilities and interests of children toward learning and endorsed the book for use by elementary teachers and teacher education students. This new book goes further; it contains scientific research expanding that previous anecdotal knowledge. My experience, although unique to me, has been intuited everywhere by attentive teachers privileged to work creatively with young children and by parents who know all too well those three lively attributes.

Research connecting physical movement and the brain has evolved and educators are cognizant of the connections. It is my hope that *Dynamic Play and Creative Movement* will make learning goals easier by providing the actual steps toward achieving these mind–body connections. I can guarantee the lessons themselves will be fun.

Acknowledgments

Accompanying the text are photographs of children involved in movement activities. Most were taken in an after-school program at P.S. 198 in New York City, sponsored by the Yorkville Youth Council in cooperation with the New York City Board of Education. The classes were led by Alice Teirstein, recent recipient of the Dance Teachers Association award. The photos, which artfully convey the spontaneity and enthusiasm of the children's response, were taken by my cousins, the late Beatrice and Jules Pinsley of New York at my request.

Photographs with captions 8.1, 9.2, 10.5, 11.3, 13.5, 17.1, and 19.2 are of children and their undergraduate student leaders of CityStep, an arts and social impact program. Pictures were taken during teacher trainings, choreography workshops, and exercises in imaginative exploration. Founded at Harvard University by Sabrina Peck, CityStep brings college students into city schools to teach personal expression and mutual understanding through dance. CityStep has now expanded to Yale, the University of Pennsylvania, Princeton, and Columbia Universities.

My gratitude to Tibor Csokasi for his wide-ranging technical support. The landscapes, seascapes, and cityscapes were photographed by Erik Unhjem, former graphics director of Ramapo College of New Jersey. Images of art works were obtained through the Open Access Program of the Metropolitan Museum of Art; the single abstraction, courtesy of artist Simon Jeruchim; the bronze figure is by me. Outdoor photographs of children engaged in dramatic pantomime were taken by me at Camp Chateaugay in Merrill, New York.

I acknowledge my appreciation to Prentice-Hall, guided by the enthusiasm of Mary Kennan who early on saw the educational importance in this work, and published Leap to the Sun: Learning through Dynamic Play. Thanks finally to my wonderful Routledge editor Amanda Savage and her competent assistant Katya Porter for always effectively being there when I needed them.

Part I

Dynamic Play

Around the world in space and time
with nothing more than a boundless imagination
and flying feet.

Figure 1.1 Boundless imagination and flying feet.

Credit line: Courtesy of Alice Teirstein.

DOI: 10.4324/9781003254812-1

1 Journey of Discovery

Creative energy, dynamic, fired by imagination—this is the energy of children. It wants to expand and reach, jump over rain puddles, fly off the house steps, leap to the sun.

The energy of children is not a quiet, internal energy; it is not geared toward receiving information and digesting facts. Concentration should therefore not be demanded as the first step in learning but the last. Concentration is pouring over loot that has been brought back to the lair of a child's mind by that artful eager scavenger imagination. Without such loot, there is really not much to get excited about.

Teachers, parents, and group leaders of children are becoming aware of this more and more. Classrooms are opening their doors, and children are spilling into the corridors, not only for space but also for breath. The corridor is freer than the classroom. Concepts in education are expanding and more room is needed to find, capture, and use our children's expansive imaginations. As it is, too much is lost out the window.

In too many homes and schools, children are still drilled in disciplines of Neatness and Order above all (the NO controls). In classrooms, children are captured and bound to desks—confining the birds to teach them why they fly. And as they sit and concentrate and learn about making nests and catching worms and landing on telephone poles, they forget just what it was they did to fly.

Ed looks out the window as the lesson drones on, idly watching the network of swaying branches, fascinated by the movement, dreaming vaguely of strength as he wonders how

DOI: 10.4324/9781003254812-2

the tree manages to stand so high, marveling that the squirrel jumps the twigs so unafraid. A swift wind carries a flurry of seeds to the ground. Birds perch, fly, land, peck at the seeds. The lesson goes on; children raise their hands and are called on. Ed watches through the window, wonders, feels excited, worries about the squirrel, does not understand so much, dreams about becoming big as a tree and fearless as a squirrel. And then the teacher calls him by name and brings him reluctantly back.

Where attention is, there the doors of learning open at a touch. When natural energy is there and used, the child does not dawdle and hesitate but rushes through to find what he is looking for.

Imagination is the key, and perception the lock to be opened. Intelligence and sensitivity, the wherewithal of learning, can then be used for all the passages to come.

Intelligence can be expanded when a child's natural energy and imagination are used as the actual machinery of learning. Reach imagination and the child's own energy will motivate the desire and through that, the ability to learn. Once the process begins, it perpetuates itself like so many other achievements of nature. It goes something like this:

- Imagination spurs investigation or trying to see.
- Seeing leads to perception. (Think of Ed and the tree and of his silent search for how the squirrel leaps with such confidence.)
- Perception leads to the desire to express what is perceived.
- Self-expression, if encouraged and well received, leads to self-confidence.
- Self-confidence leads to a continued desire to learn, to produce, and to succeed.

Dynamic Play

Imagination and energy combine in *dynamic play*, a term devised by the author to describe the creative activities presented here. Through physical participation, the children approach concepts, ideas, and familiar emotions. Using their bodies, they reach out to touch a vast world of people, animals, nature, and objects. Dynamic play is an adjunct to learning which is natural to children.

The methods and projects described provide music, art, dramatic, and dance material; natural and social science activities; games; stories; and creative physical activities of a varied nature. The spectrum of ideas relates to the world around, as well as to the world within.

Group Participation

It is best to have a group of children participating as opposed to working with a single child. A parent can invite two or three friends of the child to join in. A teacher or group leader can have the entire class participate at once or choose to divide the children into groups.

Group discussion of the ideas stimulates perception and independent thought and gives children the desire and opportunity to add their own ideas to the melting pot. As a child's own contributions are accepted and physically interpreted by the group, the child gains self-confidence. That confidence is a basic necessity of learning and crucial to creativity.

With this confidence, our hypothetical Ed is ready to think through, interpret, and expand his experiences. Then, as he makes his physical interpretation, with others or alone, he begins to acquire an intimate understanding of whatever is done—a tree spreading roots underground, a flower reaching for the sun, or a thirsty animal searching for water.

Since all the projects are based on imagery, few external supplies are required. There are no outfits, instruments, or materials to buy, and almost any available space can be used—a living room, classroom, basement, yard, or sidewalk. Dynamic play also adapts to situations in which children are already assembled. In addition to schools, this could be community centers, scout meetings, summer camps, enrichment programs, religious houses, and day-care centers.

Ways to Bring Dynamic Play into Existing Schedules

The projects are designed for children between the ages of three and eleven. Here are some of the ways dynamic play might fit into existing schedules in school, at home, in the preschool, or recreational environments:

> For a mid-morning stretch, the child or group might look out the window, feel the length of the trees and the breath of the wind, and return beside their desks to s- t- r- e- t- c- h . . . Then, drop low like the massive roots extending far in many directions below the earth and then spin high like the wind in pursuit of a dry leaf.

A science class might interpret the current experiment—flame, snakes, growth, earth alterations, the planets; a child at home can interpret a bug found hiding in the bushes and then imagine and interpret what the bug is hiding from—or just resting at home.

A history class might enact a scene from the past and bring it to life within the classroom.

Holidays and special events can be discussed, and the class can be divided into groups for separate presentation of various incidents.

A book can be interpreted or a record, a poem, a piece of music, a painting, or a sculpture—its content, form, structure, meaning.

Voices and the random sounds of life around us can be used as instruments of music or as instruments of emotional expression. Listening to those sounds of life around us can provide exciting interludes in any day and then expressing what is heard via voicing, clapping, stamping feet, running, leaping, perhaps colliding (although children can be carried away by this). To add to the experience, make a list of all the sounds children remember as they state them: a cricket, leaves rustling, a breeze, a bird chirping, water dripping, the heater humming, a sneeze, a train in the distance. Then ask each child to choose a sound to speak with their body.

The traffic of the world is brought into the room and then sent on its way. Parents, leaders, and children too will doubtlessly gather many ideas for this project suggested by their own experiences.

Dramatizing Ideas and Emotions

When an idea or strong emotion seems to crave expression, dynamic play can be invented on the spot. Let's say, Elisa is sad because she had to eat alone in the cafeteria, her friend eating with others. The class, the group, or Elisa seated at home can be led to dramatize her feelings with wilted arms, collapsing body, and dejected head movements. And if it feels silly and Elisa and her mother laugh, it will not be the first time that humor eased a fretful situation.

Suppose instead, she is angry, someone taunting or teasing her at school. A show of punching and smashing the air, swirling to land a surprise shot might work wonders at *getting back*. Far better than sitting and stewing. And laughter there helps as well. You may find children looking forward to this spontaneous deployment of energy, and the activity requested again and again.

If time and the situation permit, a regular session of dramatic dynamic play can be scheduled, with the children told to save their woes and share them at the session. The time for this can be anywhere from 10 minutes to an hour, but the more discussion and interpretation is afforded each subject, the deeper and more meaningful each will become. Frequent sessions, even short ones, are therefore an advantage. When children feel free to give expression to their feelings, they are at the same time building not only self-confidence but insight as well.

Shared Imaginations

The process will not end with Elisa or Ed, for those who lead the projects will also expand in imagination, perception, and insight. The pictures in a child's mind outwardly expressed can be helpful in many ways to an adult who sees them.

Shared imaginations make closer relationships. When you reach Ed in the area of his personal vision, communication becomes clearer. Because of your interest, his is sparked and his concentration quite naturally follows. Teaching becomes efficient because a bond has been created allowing both sides to meet on common ground. A shared mental image is a moment alive with possibilities.

Images for dynamic play need not be restricted to those suggested in this book. Adults can summon new images arising from their own backgrounds, environments, and interests. Children too will have diverse images scrambling about in their minds to offer and respond to. Those from the inner city might be unreceptive to images that intrigue their counterparts in the suburbs and the same is true in reverse. The age and sex of the participants will also influence imagery.

No matter how unusual (and perhaps awkward at first) dynamic play may appear to be, the process is natural to a child's approach to life and may prove interesting to yours.

2 Channeling Physical Energy, Imagination, and Expression

A group of children race and jump and scamper on a field, running, yelling, having a good time. If you did not know any of them personally you might laugh at their antics, enjoying their carefree play. But if you did know them, you would be aware of the one who held back slightly or the one who shouted loudest or the one who always managed to overrun the others. Aware as children are aware, for in the midst of their collective play, each child feels quite different from the others, quite special. And each is indeed different and special, for contained within the universal qualities that make children so typical are the very elements that serve to make them each unique. A careful look, therefore, at what these exuberant little people have in common might reveal the qualities that make them each so individual. These universal characteristics are

- physical energy,
- imagination,
- motivation for expression.

The first and most noticeable common characteristic is an abundance of physical energy. If a stretch of road should appear before them, they will run it; if a leg should dangle under them, they will swing it; and anyone who has been within reverberating distance of a child or has been kicked accidentally in the shin by one will testify to that.

The second common characteristic is a vigorous imagination. Imagination is running at full stride at a time when

DOI: 10.4324/9781003254812-3

attention span and the ability to reason are just entering the starting gate.

The third universal characteristic is a strong motivation for expression, each child in a personal way.

All these qualities are natural endowments, and like other endowments of nature, they serve a function. Children are, after all, relatively new on the scene with a lot ahead of them to learn. With physical energy, imagination, and the urge to express themselves, they have the basic equipment to begin making their way.

The equipment will not serve them as well as it might, however, if we adults do not recognize these qualities as natural endowments and, as a consequence, neglect to give them the attention they deserve: the attention we give to the endowments of intellect, talent, and beauty, for example. Too often it is only the enthusiasm with which these properties are displayed that attracts our attention. Some of the most frequent requests man makes to his begotten child are:

- "Stop doing that!"
- "Stop fooling around!"
- "Stop that racket!"

The first command refers to Ed's physical energy; the second, to his imagination; and the third, to his desire to express himself. Since we all have made these wailful cries, it would seem that self-preservation alone might urge us not to fight but join, not stop the inevitable traffic nor even slow it but direct it.

It can be done for these "noisy" qualities of children are not only universal but strong enough within each child to be used dynamically in education. By education I mean enlightenment, whether it be at home, school, or play.

When Ed is directed to use his physical vitality to interpret what he observes and learns, his experience and understanding expand. He thus participates in events that occurred before he was born, in places he has never seen; he brings his own sensations and emotions and those of others participating with him to a level where he can consciously explore

Figure 2.1 Energy can be channeled.

Credit line: Courtesy of Alice Teirstein.

them. He shares in the wonders of birth, growth, and change in the world around him.

When Ed is encouraged in his self-expression and made to feel that what he has to say is valid, he will likely continue to express himself in maturity. Expression, no matter how eager in childhood, subdues as the magnitude of the world is confronted. But if Ed has developed means of expression while the motivation was strong, and if he has acquired that confidence in himself so vital to communication, he will not be overawed but stimulated by what confronts him in maturity.

Finally, if Ed's vivid imagination can be retained as the sensitive inner eye it surely is, it can serve as his guide throughout life, leading him to beauty and truth as faithfully as a German shepherd leads its blind master across a myriad of streets to home. Imagination, more so than any other facet of childhood, deserves discussion and consideration, perhaps because it is quiet and easily drowned out in the noise and confusion of a busy world, and perhaps because understanding its significance may give rise to forms of expression found in the arts and sciences, which will serve the child through to adulthood. But most of all, I think, because from this imagination will eventually emerge the individual— thoughtful, perceptive, and awakened.

Dynamic play is a term devised by the author to synthesize the learning that presents itself dynamically when children's active imagination, physical energy, and urgency for self-expression are combined in programmed creative activity. Dynamic play is an adjunct to learning that is natural to children. The ways by which it can be used to import the broad ideas of the outer world into the inner lives of children in their regular home and school learning is the subject of this book.

3 Imagination

Origin of Individuality

Imagination might be said to be an inner vision, a private way of seeing. As a very young child, Elise uses this vision to face the world around her. Size is no help, intellectual acumen is undeveloped, past experiences are few, and opportunities for new ones depend on other people. Her imagination, however, is vast and all her own and depends on no one.

Imagination provides answers to questions too complex even to be formulated in an untutored mind. Elise as an infant looking at the grass beside her blanket on the lawn knows nothing about grass, but she is absorbed in touching it, watching the blades bend and spring back. Imagination answers her silent curiosity. At 2, she might fill the night's darkness with monsters because she does not understand the sounds she hears, the shadows she sees. Send her at 3 to fetch something for you, and on the way, she will have a dozen or more "adventures," each involving her every sense, all originating from her imagination. She has no sense of time for that is too real, so do not hope to have the object at hand in a hurry. Between the ages of 3 and 11, imagination and reason coordinate as needs arise: the less Elise knows, the more she imagines, and the more she knows, the less need for her private source of information. This balance is true in a more complicated way throughout life for those who are not satisfied with answers are usually those with keen imaginations, continually searching even as their scope of knowledge increases.

"That child has a terrific imagination!" the mother sighs. She is right in observing this, but what she may not appreciate

DOI: 10.4324/9781003254812-4

is that every child has a terrific imagination. It is a natural resource for learning and discovery that at present is not sufficiently tapped. Imagination in the young child is well developed at a time when mental processes are just being formed, yet teaching efforts are directed overwhelmingly toward the mental processes of concentration, reason, and coordination.

Because children have an expert ability to form vivid mental pictures for new facts and information, there are many things they might learn with the help of imagery that might be harder to manage cognitively. An example of this is teaching very young children to dress themselves. Where it might be difficult to remember and coordinate the sequence of movements required to accomplish this feat, using an image makes the procedure clear. For example, putting on a shirt: here lives a big bear in a little house. His head pops out the chimney and his arms poke out the windows, one on each side. Putting on trousers: a squirmy caterpillar (the foot) travels through a long tunnel (the trouser leg), wriggling along until finally out he comes at the other end. The examples of course are endless, as endless as the creative mind. What is important in these games is this: When children can make such daily accomplishments at an early age, confidence in their competence begins at that early age, and they are receptive and eager for what's around the corner.

Discipline too is often difficult with threats and admonitions but is both easy and effective through imagery. A scenario for getting a young child to pick up her toys is offered in Chapter 8. In summary, this is it: "Clean up this room instantly!" is a command allowing for nothing but compliance or battle, but the fanciful announcement, "Mrs. Wigglebottom is coming to tea. . . . Hurry, we're serving in this very room!" not only puts fun into a dismal chore but also gives the child a very real motivation to clean the room. And this despite the fact that the situation is unreal. After all, the reason one tidies a room is so it will look nice, but to a child, it looks just as nice messy. Therefore, if the child tidies it, it is done for no other reason than that the parent ordered it.

But serving tea to Mrs. Wigglebottom—like any guest, no matter with a wiggly bottom as the mother had aptly demonstrated—the room has got to be straight for that!

The value of learning through imagery is not simply to make learning easier and more effective (which it accomplishes) but to cause learning from the earliest age to be the joyful habit it should certainly be. Our Elise, familiar with seeing and using and valuing the pictures in her mind, is awake to the changing pictures all around her—to read, to ask, to be curious, and to seek to understand. Her confidence grows that she is good at learning. This feeling of success and anticipation of more success is a fertile field for the academic learning that will come later.

We tend to be more aware of Elise's involvement with imagination as a young child because she talks aloud to herself and so tells us a bit about what's going on inside those closed doors. But children from five to eleven are also focusing on their private inner worlds, forming pictures and impressions in their minds, and for these they usually make no verbal explanations. Yet pictures are there that can be defined, expanded, and shared when knowledgeable and caring adults are nearby. Reaching those inner worlds creates an opportunity to sharpen an adult's learning or to expand and deepen a relationship.

Imagination plays a lesser role in the activities of children beyond the age of 11, but it would be interesting to know how much they profited from the imagination of earlier years. Too often it was not directed during those vital years, used only as play matter for games and when the need for games was outgrown, became little used. But how wonderful it would be if that childhood imagination at the very height of its powers could be channeled into a specific area that could itself be expanded with age and maturity.

The area most suited to this is the visual or performing arts. Together with the child's natural physical energy and zeal for acquiring new skills, it could form a foundation to build on not only for the fulfillment that creativity affords but also for a meaningful appreciation of the creative product itself.

If a child can be given exposure to the arts by participating in them in the early years, how much easier it will be to relate to them in maturity. We all have felt an awakening of imagination through provocative theater or music or dance and, at one time or another, have been stimulated by a painting or a work of sculpture. Perhaps we have wanted to become involved in creating something ourselves but through lack of personal exposure did not know where to begin. As adults, there are many experiences we are afraid to attempt. Our consciousness of self is too strong. We have organized our resources—our capabilities and limitations, our strengths and weaknesses—into columns and totaled them, secure in this but somewhat immobilized as well. Most important, we sense that something is missing, and it is. For the enjoyment of art is not only aesthetic appreciation. It is the affirmation of one's individuality. Seeing something of beauty, of sensual impact, or of spiritual importance—recognizing it as such with one's own eyes and valuing it with one's own standards—is the essence of individuality.

We live in an age of visual communications in social media, magazines, television, billboards, movies—and bombarded with the images of what we are told is beauty. Our eyes and senses become trained by advertising agencies whose giant commercial imaginations dwarf our own. Finding a chubby, rosy-cheeked woman more attractive than a pale, slender blonde or finding a stronger peace in working than lying in the sun puts premium value on personal vision. If our individuality yields to advertised beauty, we have nothing to counter this with and must accept it as truth.

Imagination, the backbone of individuality, must be developed with the same effort that is applied to the development of the mind and the body. For the more imagination is valued and used profitably in childhood, the more confidence we will have that it can be trusted in maturity.

One final thought on the topic of this chapter though not the theme of this book. Teenage angst is real, as are the consequences. Imagination can be painfully acute in teenagers at a time when social and emotional needs are profound, coupled with unfamiliar academic demands and self-exposure.

Figure 3.1 Shared imaginations make beautiful relationships.
Credit line: Courtesy of Alice Teirstein.

How helpful it might then be for a child to have felt comfortable all along in sharing his imaginings with an accepting adult and open to their reasoning.

60 Boys

Some years ago in the spring, I brought a small group of dance students to entertain disturbed children at the Rockland Psychiatric Center in Orangeburg, New York. We had expected a female audience as had been the case once before, but instead, we were greeted by 60 somber-faced boys, ranging in age from 7 to 15. It portended doomsday for the 12 little girls in our "troop" who had come with visions of flowers in their heads.

A quick narrow-eyed, face-to-face look told us we had better make allies of these boys, or we would be shelled if not with tomatoes, which were not yet in season, then with a heavy silence, equally painful. A few lively songs were sung. Then paper and crayons were given out, and the boys were asked to draw pictures of spring, which they did, the older boys were reluctant to start until seeing the pictures emerging from the younger ones and it became a competition. The girls collected the drawings and studied them, looking for elements of spring that they could interpret.

The girls divided into groups and quickly planned their improvisations after which one child from each group announced what was to be done. There was no selection or rejection of the boys' pictures. Enough of the elements of spring were repeated in the pictures to make it possible to use all the boys' ideas. Such things as robins, grass, trees, kites, birds, flowers, and baseball were interpreted, and the boys recognized the subjects that came from their drawings.

Our second project, in view of the season, was colored Easter eggs. The boys suggested various colors and then were called on to guess the color being interpreted after each improvisation. Colors are subjective in feeling, but they have associations that are universal, particularly among children: yellow is bright like the sun and red is happy like rosebuds and Santa Claus or violent like blood and fire. Then lines and patterns for the eggs were suggested, such as zigzag and polka dots and curves and circles, and these, too, were interpreted through movement and guessed at by the boys.

Third on the program was a discussion of the many different forms that water can take. The boys named several: rain, hail, rivers, ice, waterfalls, oceans, fountains, and so on. Then, without naming them in advance, some of these were interpreted, and the boys tried to guess which they were by the movements. Next, things that go together, such as ball and bat, or things that are foils for each other, such as the spider and the fly, were talked about and interpreted. Again, all the ideas came from the audience.

The procedure throughout was that the boys raised their hands to suggest ideas and to guess as I walked among them. The eagerness to participate became so great and the contact between us so strong that many times my hand was grabbed or the boys stood, waving both arms. As the afternoon progressed, they shouted their answers without waiting to be called and we dispensed with that formality. When our program had ended, the boys wanted to "play some of the games" themselves. Much of the program was then repeated as they participated with their own movements while the girls and I guessed. There were a few boys who sat it out. They said that what they really wanted to do was not the spider and the fly but disco with the girls. We knew we couldn't win em all.

This event took place several years ago and more contemporary images and stories from digital media would need to be used now. But when we left that afternoon, we knew that something new and important had happened to most of the boys in that room. It is fairly certain that few if any of them had any previous background or familiarity with this kind of movement or a structured reach for creative ideas. All had emotional problems, and most were culturally deprived as well. It is possible that some of the boys had never seen a lake or a rabbit, although they drew these things in their pictures. But all of them that day had looked beyond themselves to try to see and within themselves to try to understand.

There was a feeling of importance in the air. Their ideas had been accepted by and responded to by other children (girls, no less!) and something beautiful was made from them. Equally important, they had discovered an Aladdin's lamp within their grasp: a way to think and to imagine; a way to produce something akin to art; a way to express, communicate, and grow.

4   Getting Started

The approach and projects in the book are designed for teachers, group leaders, and parents of children of various ages from 3 to 11 years of age. As such, their use is suitable in preschools, grade schools, after-school groups, camps, scouting groups, and in the home with one or more children present. The purpose is to give recognition to the substantial natural endowments that young children possess and utilize that awareness in the promotion of productive and joyful learning.

Imagination, physical energy, and the urgency for self-expression are three qualities that are universally dominant in children. Amazingly, these qualities, each of which is a dynamic energy, are not used sufficiently in education. Yet when these natural qualities are tapped into, they can serve to increase children's perception, awareness of the world around them, and understanding of themselves in relation to that world. Through imagination, children can visualize new ideas and project themselves into a spectrum of unfamiliar situations. With abundant energy, the child can physically interpret what is observed, thereby viscerally expanding experience and understanding. With the urgency for personal expression, the child is motivated toward interest in the arts. The arts, whether it is music, visual art, theater, dance, or writing lead on to the continual pursuit of understanding oneself in relation to the outside world.

Projects described in the text and the methods to participate in them involve the natural and social sciences; holidays; sports; industry; nature; animals; emotions; creative

DOI: 10.4324/9781003254812-5

activities in music, art, drama, and dance; and a plethora of ideas that bounce off these.

All the projects are based on imagery and require no supplies; therefore, they can be adapted to any situation where children meet. The projects are presented in an informal, nontechnical style and designed for men and women with no special training in either leading or participating in physical activity programs.

Part I emphasizes the value of childhood imagination, physical energy, and the need for personal expression in the learning process. Explained is the concept of teaching through imagery. Methods and procedures are given for using the projects in a variety of situations where children gather.

Part II contains research relating the connection of physical movement to brain activity. A chapter on the developing brain offers an awe-inspiring glimpse into the unfathomable resources of the brain that are available when used, followed by an overview of brain development, and concluding with how brain activity interrelates with creative movement and dance to enhance both brain and body.

Part III contains 50 creative projects relating to movements of various parts of the body. These projects encourage children to use their bodies with confidence as an instrument of expression. Simple directions are given that enable leaders to make effective use of the material.

Part IV consists of 90 projects carefully planned to expose children to a range of provocative ideas and activities. Through active group discussion exploring the ideas followed by physical interpretations, children gain an awakening interest and keener awareness of each subject. Moreover, each child's comments during the discussions, because they are acknowledged and often followed by group action, can lead to a growth of confidence in the *value* of their feelings and observations, a confidence that is projected to other areas of learning.

Part V contains 15 stories with suggestions for using them in the classroom. Each story can be read aloud and improvised upon as a separate group activity. Several together can also serve as entertainment for an audience of children by children. Because of the imagery and related vocabulary, teachers and parents might find the stories stimulating reading exercises for 7- to 10-year-old children and as read-aloud stories for younger children.

A Word to Parents

The projects in the following pages are given with procedures for the classroom or group situation. Nevertheless, almost all the projects and improvisations in Parts III and IV can be done informally with as few as two people—you and the child. They can be done among brothers and sisters and playmates and incidentally will also provide interesting activities for birthday parties.

The stories in Part V use a great deal of imagery and can simply be read to a child or a child can read them alone with no further interpretation. Since the ideas are essentially visual, the child will form mental images for the characters and the plot. You can suggest that some pictures be drawn for the stories (a quieter kind of interpretation and very good for a rainy day).

When the term *leader* is used in this book, it refers to whomever and wherever the children are being led. Certain sections of the text will not apply directly to the home situation but may provide insight into other possibilities of the project that you can develop for your own use. If there is an instrument of any kind in the house producing sound, it can inspire combinations involving music and ideas. Music of various kinds, recorded, instrumental, or percussive, can add to the projects, but discussing the ideas and interpreting them together are the essential activities involved.

Definitions

Leader: The term *leader* applies to anyone leading children in an activity, be it parent, teacher, babysitter, scout leader, counselor, therapist, grandma, or grandpa.

He or she: When *he* or *she* are used in reference to leaders or children, it is for simplicity of sentence structure and intends inclusion of all genders.

Ages of the children: Many of the same projects can be adapted for younger or older children, and it is left to the discretion of the leaders which to use for their groups.

The prearranged signal: To get the attention of a large group of children during the action it is helpful to arrange a signal in advance, such as when the leader's hand goes up, all voices and movement stop immediately and every hand goes up so others can see. The signal should be practiced several times before the projects get underway. Have the children make loud noises in advance of the signal coming, and then see how instantaneously they can become silent when your hand is raised. Trust that when enthusiasm rises and adjacent class teachers start banging on the walls, this signal will be useful.

5 Questions and Answers

For the Leader

Q: Are people who are comfortable with children but untrained in physical activity capable of leading a program of this kind?

A: Yes. There are no formal techniques for leaders to teach and therefore none to learn. The primary objective is to support children's participation in the ideas through movement, not to teach movement per se. The only training involved (and this applies to both leaders and children) is guiding imagination to express itself in physical ways. This is effected on an individual basis, all participants in their own way.

Q: Must a leader be physically agile to conduct such a group?

A: No. An agile leader might have more fun jumping into the projects full throttle, but a leader not able to get up easily from the floor (like me) can be just as successful (ask a child to demonstrate). None of the projects require special agility. Leaders at any age, with understanding of their body's capabilities, can use the material. Success depends not on physical dexterity but on imagination, enthusiasm, and interest. But when dexterity is limited rely on an agile child or two to demonstrate the movement explained.

Q: Are the methods and descriptions comprehensible to those totally unfamiliar with this type of activity?

DOI: 10.4324/9781003254812-6

A: Yes. All the projects are described with imagery and associated words, not counts and diagrams. No technical language is used.

Q: Is it natural for a leader to feel self-conscious and insecure?

A: Yes, especially in the beginning, as in any new venture. Some of the movements may appear unnatural, but this is because they are unfamiliar. Actually what is more unnatural is the fact that we use the body so little considering its versatility. (Witness the Hindu Yogi and the Egyptian belly dancer for versatility.) Remember that to the children, most of the movements will appear completely natural. They are used to doing "odd" things with their bodies and, after an initial hesitancy wondering what it's all about, will welcome you for providing it. Since they presumably will be your only critics, there is no reason to feel self-conscious. Just be sure no one is taking pictures.

For the Children

Q: Is dynamic play or creative movement more suitable for girls than for boys?

A: No. The idea that this kind of activity might interfere with a boy's batting average exists in some quarters but is fallacious. Boys are eager to express themselves through movement when the subject matter interests them. They are, in addition, eager to show off physically. As long as they are made to feel confident in themselves, they will not defect to Little League. Because of some existing prejudice in this area, they might require more encouragement than girls do to achieve this confidence, but the results are worth the effort.

Q: Is creative movement or dynamic play a course in interpretive dance?

A: No. One of Webster's definitions of *dance*—"To move nimbly and merrily"—applies most certainly to the program since this is the way children react to it, but dancing is not the objective. The purpose is to give each child a means of self-expression, openness to ideas, and ways to communicate those ideas. And what better tool to use than the body you carry with you? The exposure to movement may lead some children to pursue dance, but they might just as easily become interested in sculpture, painting, music, or other endeavors revealed to them by the program.

Q: Will children totally unfamiliar with dynamic play be able to relate to it?

A: Yes. Dynamic play is unfamiliar to children in name only. The substance of the program is quite familiar and the movements themselves, described in terms of familiar images, are equally easy to respond to.

What Should Accompany the Movement?

A drum of some kind is useful, not only to assist in the spirit of the projects but also to override the clamor of children expressing themselves. It makes for more organized noise and can sound impressive in the halls. Whether or not you have ever drummed before does not matter since the gist of it is acquired by doing it, a tribal instinct perhaps. There may be children in the group who prefer drumming to actively participating. This is quite acceptable and can even be encouraged after the children have become accustomed to working as a group.

Children can also provide accompaniment by humming, singing, or clapping. This works best while the children are watching others rather than when they are moving themselves. A piano is a lovely thing to have, as is a pianist, in which case music can be improvised on the spot. Tapes are helpful to keep on hand as well. A list of musical resources that are suitable is included at the end of the book but leaders might have multiple resources accessible already on their smart phones in both melody and song.

Figure 5.1 "Dance—To move nimbly and merrily" (Webster).
Credit line: Courtesy of Alice Teirstein.

The voice of the leader, notwithstanding, is the most effective instrument for setting the mood and pace and providing the impetus for movement. This is the only instrument really required. If the children start out their participation in dynamic play having only the leader's voice as accompaniment, they may be content just with that. In their minds the band may already be playing; there seems to be some element of rhythmic activity going on in the heads of most children. Watch them swinging their legs under the table or tapping pencils on the desks. The apparatus is turned on "automatic" early in the morning and plays away all day long.

What Kind of Shoes or Clothes Should Be Worn?

Depending on the type of floor—its texture or its cleanliness—dynamic play can be done in shoes or bare feet. If the floor is slippery, moving in stocking feet is not advised. Shoes inhibit movement somewhat and socks don't allow one to get a grip on the floor, so although moving in bare feet is best, most situations are not conducive to this. Therefore, try for bare feet but since the goals of the program center as much on mind and heart, wearing shoes, galoshes, or hip boots can be made to work.

A cautionary word about the procedure of removing socks and shoes when you are able to do so among preschoolers. Have each child tuck socks into the shoes and bring them to a far wall, out of the way, observing where they've been put. Many a happy child walks off with one sock missing and shoes a size too big. All things considered, if the child ends up with the right shoes on the wrong feet, you've had a good day!

The regular clothes children wear to school are fine for moving about the floor and room. Removing sweaters and jackets before starting is always a good idea.

Get Going

So now it is time to begin. Gather your ideas, taking as many projects intact from the book as you wish and embellishing others with your personal knowledge of your child or group. Then, remove your jacket, nod casually to your peers as they pass you carrying your drum (or in your stockinged feet), and try to act as if you know what you're doing. In other words, wing it. The children will take it from there.

Part II

Movement and Brain Connections

6 Brain Plasticity and Exercise

The child prancing around in your living room or actively engaged in your classroom has come to you factory-installed with a remarkable set of endowments, much of it related to natural energy and the imaginative ways he or she can put it to use. It is likely that a portion of those attributes are yours as well or you would not have picked up this book. You are probably accustomed to expressing yourself in some innovative, forward-looking way.

Most certainly you have seen the imperative to move that your child or those in your care exhibits, running whenever space permits or swinging a leg under the table when it doesn't. And you've become aware that research on brain activity supports what you intuitively knew all along: a correlation between all that movement and brain activity. Indeed, new research puts more emphasis than ever on the relationship between physical activity and learning from the very first few months of life onward.

Accepting that there exist distinct body–mind connections associated with those children cavorting so rakishly in your living room or classroom is the first step. Learning how to use the resource of physical energy towards making them more eager for learning than they already are is next. Understanding some of the research behind the body–mind principle will then hopefully give you the confidence to move *dynamically* right along with the kids.

Neural Networks and the Mind–Body Linkage

Brain plasticity is the term describing the ability of the brain to learn and store information, the ability to modify its

DOI: 10.4324/9781003254812-8

connections or rewire itself. Movement, whether in the form of exercise or physical play, stirs neural activity in the brain which helps to support brain plasticity.

Neural networks—connections between neurons—form with active physical movement, a natural process that helps the brain to learn and remember. In addition to exercise enhancing brain functionality by making these synaptic connections, there exist the consequences that relate to lack of exercise. Research reveals that being more sedentary than active increases bodily fatigue (ironically, the antithesis of energy expenditure). And with lethargy may come a feeling of boredom, which itself inhibits energy—an energy that learning requires. Added to this negative mush is the possibility of obesity which is exacerbated by a sedentary lifestyle. This poses a serious threat to health in general.

Evidence of the linkage between mind and body has today become a groundswell, writes Eric Jenson in his book *Teaching with the Brain in Mind (2005)*, adding, "Most neuroscientists agree that movement and cognition are powerfully connected." Tracing the pathways of brain activity, it appears evident that "the part of the brain that processes movement is the same part of the brain that processes learning." The author describes the relationship between the vestibular (inner ear) and cerebellar (motor activity) system, as an "interaction that helps us keep our balance, turn thoughts into actions and coordinate movements." Even playground activities that stimulate inner ear motion have proved helpful to learning.

The Mayo Clinic, in its effort to both combat obesity and encourage active learning, has undertaken to design classrooms that would ensure the physical movement of its young inhabitants, as opposed to their sitting for hours trapped at their desks. Much of the research of the Mayo Clinic is directed toward adding exercise to children's school day, such as stretching and the like, or various furniture setups to encourage walking around the classroom from place to place.

But how much more rewarding for mind and body to be engaged together via a creative movement session filling the room instead: Drumbeats carried by some, foot-stamping and clapping by others, a musical tape playing to inspire heads and bodies and limbs as the classroom shakes with energy. Everyone in motion. Teacher too. Imagine that!

Eric Jenson's research argues that beyond the fact that exercise fuels the brain with oxygen, it also feeds it neurotrophins, which increase the connections between neurons. This growth in neural connections leads to increased cognition, memory, and even the reduced likelihood of depression. Some studies revealed an improvement in social skills with exercise, others better academic performance and attitude toward school. Play involving physical movement, which most play does, is shown to increase cognition. (Jenson 2020).

Healthy, active kids make better learners. We are not designed to sit. We are designed to move. Dr. John Medina, author of *Brain Rules* (2nd ed., 2014) argues for more universal understanding of the brain, in particular accommodating our routines and the spaces we design for learning and working, with how the brain actually works and thrives. He cites five ingredients involved in children's intelligence, worthy of parental recognition: "The desire to explore, self-control, creativity, verbal communication, and interpreting nonverbal communication" (p. 100). As he expands on these traits, I see dynamic play involved in all of them, from the initial group discussions through the exploration of ideas via movements to the interpretation of concepts through thoughtful improvisations.

The CDC (Centers for Disease Control and Prevention) is much in the news at this writing while we are still under threat of COVID-19 and its variants. Its in-depth study completed as far back as 2003, the National Youth Risk Behavior Study (YRBS), revealed that the lack of exercise and movement had a distinctly negative effect on learning and education: markedly lower grades reflecting poor learning capabilities.

Stephen Demers in *Mind, Brain, Health & Education,* summarizing research by the Mayo Clinic in 2010, writes: "Forcing learners to remain sedentary is counterintuitive to the learning process and health of learners. We now have evidence that compels us to make changes for classroom movement. We owe it to students today and students of future generations."

David A. Sousa, in his book *How the Brain Learns* (2016), writes about the effects of movement and dance on the brain. He finds that even short, moderate physical exercise improves brain performance, explaining further that regular physical activity increases the number of capillaries in the brain, thus facilitating blood transport. Exercise also increases the amount of oxygen in the blood, which significantly enhances cognitive performance. He argues that teachers need to encourage more movement in all classrooms at all grade levels, that movement activities are also effective because they involve more sensory input, hold the students' attention for longer periods of time, help them make connections between new and past learning and improve long-term recall.

Sousa and other researchers on the brain note the need for children, wired as so many are to technology, to focus better on the data to process it, and take the time for self-reflection to absorb the meanings. In dynamic play, group discussion about children's perceptions precedes the physical interpretations. This formulation of ideas followed by an acceptance of the ideas by others builds self-confidence, a vital element in the motivation for learning and the subsequent garnering of the ability to focus.

Debby Mitchell in this excerpt from her book *Learning through Movement and Music* (GeoMotion Group assembled by Jean Blaydes 2012), writes:

> Exercise benefits the brain even before it benefits the body. The brain does not store its own fuel nor does it produce its own fuel. The brain relies on the body to get this—oxygen and glucose—to the brain. The healthier

and more physically fit the body is, the more efficiently the brain functions. This is because exercise changes the brain at a molecular level by:

Growing new brain cells, a process called neurogenesis.
Producing BDNF (brain-derived neurotropic factor), nicknamed the fertilizer for the brain.
Strengthening secondary dendritic branching that increases memory retrieval.
Improving mood by balancing the neurotransmitters: endorphins, dopamine, cortisol, and serotonin. (Mitchell 2012)

The brain is a complex structure. More parts of the brain "light up" or are used when a person is moving or physically active. Exercise creates the optimal environment for neural plasticity, the ability of the brain to change. Exercise puts the brain and body into balance naturally by regulating brain chemicals that control mood and responses to stress. Research on the brain reveals how exercise can aid in learning and cognition (Ratey 2008).

The Mitchell/Blaydes excerpt continues, included here for the breath of coverage it offers together with attributed acknowledgments:

Improved Brain Function

- Increased capacity for learning with the growth of an estimated 9,000 cells (neurons) daily.
- Increased neurons in the hippocampus, the learning and memory center of the brain. [The neocortex recently known to be more active.]
- Protection of brain functions for increased health.
- Increased connections among existing neural pathways.
- Increased brain organization and integration.

(Medina 2014)

Enhanced Cognition

The objective was to examine the impact that either acute or long-term exercise has on cognition.

- Enhanced mental performance, memory, learning, attention, decision making, and multitasking.
- Increased adaptivity, efficiency, and ability to reorganize neural pathways based on new experiences.
- Increased executive function to enhance higher-level mental skills that inhibit impulses, shift focus, control emotions, initiate, plan, organize, and monitor.
- Improved arousal and vigilance that in educational terms translates to focus.
- Improved perception.
- Improved cellular function (learning translates from short-term to long-term memory and learning becomes automatic).
- Decreased distraction.
- Improved process of putting thought into action.
- Improved ability to put patterns into sequences (letters into words, words into sentences).

(Etnier et al. 1997)

Improved Memory

- Enhanced short-term working memory and increased long-term potentiality.
- Physiological strengthening of the brain as the result of dendritic branching.
- Staved-off symptoms and signs of dementia.

Reduced Stress

- Reduced test anxiety.
- Decreased symptoms of depression after just three days of exercise.

- Improved adaptation to challenges in a changing environment.
- Decreased toxic effects of high levels of stress.
- Reduced neuronal death caused by chronic stress.

Balanced Mood and Behavior

- Improved attention, motivation, self-esteem, cooperation.
- Ameliorated learned helplessness.
- Improved resilience and self-confidence.
- Increased ability to withstand stress and frustration.
- Fewer behavior problems.
- Increased coping skills when presented with a new situation.
- Increased self-discipline and self-esteem.
- Reduction or elimination of the need for ADHD [attention-deficit/hyperactivity disorder] medications and antidepressants.
- Regulated mood through the natural balance of neurotransmitters.
- Regulated sleep patterns for increased alertness during school hours.
- Intrinsic sense of reward, motivation, and satisfaction.
- Impulse control.
- Joyful attitude.
- Increased state of happiness and life satisfaction.

Improved Social Skills and Behavior

- Lower levels of drug use in teens.
- Better family relationships.
- Improved attention, impulsivity, motivation, self-esteem, and cooperation.

Improved Academic Performance

The objective of this study was to examine the association of scholastic performance with physical activity and fitness of children.

- Improved reading and math scores.
- Improved reading comprehension and analysis.
- Higher IQ scores.
- Higher grade-point average in adolescents.
- Enhanced creativity.
- Intensified focus in classroom.
- Improved problem-solving skills.
- Reduced truancy and dropout rates.

(Dwyer et al. 2001)

Perception and Intelligence

As an overview, what can physical movement, if used in productive ways, accomplish? Could it, for one, increase perception in a child, and would that be helpful to learning? The short answer is yes and yes.

The perceptive child, the child looking and reacting to things around her becomes practiced at being alert and interested. Encouraged to perceive what is seen, heard, touched, tasted, or smelled she is moved to respond and make connections. "Look how the wind moves the tree branches. Where does the wind come from? How tall the trees are! What keeps them up? Listen to the sounds the birds make. Are they talking? What makes this flower smell so nice? Why does a skunk smell so funny?" Neural connections in the brain are made as these associative connections are voiced and the more made and responded to, the more the child is stimulated to make. The correlation between cognition and burgeoning intelligence is not hard to miss.

When perception is followed by some questioning response, something is produced: an awareness, an understanding, an idea. Perhaps, going further, an object of art or craft is produced from the idea, or a song or dance. Whether perception summons ideas, chatter, pictures, poems, concoctions, rhythms, or castles in the sand, as years go on the child will search for more sophisticated resources to express what she feels or to solve a problem, academic or every day. Finding resources to meet needs will be a way of life, a search to discover that becomes an ongoing quest as ever more questions arise to engage her.

Self-Confidence and Learning

Self-confidence is a key factor in learning at any age but is particularly important in the early years. No one can respect the validity of what he or she perceives without self-confidence. Seeing becomes enlightening perception only through self-confidence, through placing *value* on one's observations. Because of this, the development of perception and self-confidence must be simultaneous.

There is little doubt that parental influence on this crucial development is a distinctive one. So too is the influence of others, particularly siblings, although the natural hierarchy that comes with birth order seems acceptable to children. (The younger seems to expect getting brow-beaten by the elder and adapts a temperament to go along, usually a darn good one.)

Additionally, helpers, neighbors, classmates, and teachers can exert effects on self-confidence even through sporadic incidents, sometimes detrimental. These in many instances cannot be avoided. Helping children develop a solid sense of self to withstand the inevitable blows to it is crucial. Children need to understand that their actions will at times be faulty, but they are individuals who can be in control of their actions and make decisions to change them. To feel themselves weak, bad, incompetent, clumsy, foolish, ridiculous, incorrigible, or stupid is to weaken trust in themselves at its very foundation, making it harder to counteract mistakes. Deprecating words like those may seem to be sloughed off by a child, but they take hold. In addition to the crushing self-image they impose on the psyche, the attitudes behind them become an obstacle to overcome just at the time in their lives when there are so many rich new experiences to reach for.

Self-efficacy is the term behavioral psychologists use to describe the sense of competence we develop that helps us deal with life's ups and downs. The confidence that we will be able to cope with whatever challenges life throws at us is vital to our ability to function well and to regulate our plethora of disturbing moods and emotions. Moreover, without this confidence, our natural motivation to focus on learning new things diminishes.

The effort to enhance a child's emotional well-being is sometimes overlooked given the many routines that encompass a day. Tasks at hand will take priority, mistakes and rebukes will occur and recur, the child's emotional reactions buried under the constraints of time and too much going on. But if cumulatively these emotional responses surface as universally negative in the child's perception, self-flagellation can crush the burgeoning individualism sprouting like the first daisies of spring. Building a foundation of self-worth is a bedrock against those debilitating situations sure to come.

Encouraging kids to productively use what they already have plenty of—physical energy, imagination, and self-expression—can enhance that sense of well-being because this they do well and they know it. When a kid feels he's good at something, he feels pretty good about himself. When things feel balanced from within without excessive anger or resentment or confusion, she is free to reach outward to take things in. Her brain is receptive to learning. It's a no-brainer.

Starting at the Start

Surely all five senses of sight, hearing, smell, touch, and taste seem to be in overdrive in the early months of life. Indeed, babies seem programmed to exercise every attribute in their arsenal. Well, babies do not have reasoning or logic at their disposal and their size is little help; survival depends, instead, on external care and the use of those attributes. They must let you know what's wrong and what they're up to by their laughter and their tears and their bodies in motion.

The physical energy of toddlers and preschoolers can drive adults nuts at times, but that energy is the generator that sets everything in motion. The verbal expressiveness of young children can be equally exasperating in the vitality of their urgencies, their questions, their demands. Still, accepting all that physical and verbal ruckus as evidence of the inborn endowments of childhood can be a helpful attitude. The next step is to set out to channel it.

As the months and years go by, the task is to find opportunities and activities to expand those attributes. Talking about what you see and discover together as you explore ideas smooths out the wrinkles. And as you share the journey, you are giving her confidence to voice more observations, stimulating ever more connective pathways in the brain.

What a road you are on! You, too, for your brain also is making connections, as it does throughout your life. If her questions and observations provoke you to see something in a new way, your sensory apparatus is sending an arsenal of neurons to other areas in your brain, feeding your capacity to latch on to new learning and to hold on to the information you have in the complex arena of your memory. The brain builds on the experiences you've given it to predict your next moves and keep you safe. We all have a built-in *mother* (as I've come to think of it), our brains keeping track of our moves and giving us the help we need in the form of billions of neurons and chemical transmitters that spark with the energy of neural pathways busy wiring, connecting, seeking patterns, and making new ones. We are scarcely aware of all the lively commotion going on in there, all the while we make our thoughtful moves.

Continuing to find opportunities to engage our children's physical and expressive energies in the grade-school years is easy to do by choosing activities both in and out of school that encourage mental stimulation and quiet reflection. This is a nice combination for emotional balance.

In adolescence, a teen might be guided into distinctive creative art forms as his interests become more focused. The pursuits of creative writing, music, visual art, theater, and dance rely on those same natural attributes of childhood: curiosity, imagination, energy, and the need for personal expression. Responsiveness to the expression of others as a spectator is happily added to the mix.

While you are feeding her brain with these opportunities to expand learning and experience and the emotions that accompany them, you are building memories. Emotions are closely connected to long-term memory through the limbic systems where emotions are housed. My mother at the age of 101 remembered her father taking her to the opera as a child—not her older, more beautiful sister but she whom her father criticized as having "a long nose." She remembers around the same time begging for a new coat, ashamed to wear the one in tatters to school. The memories coalesced: the rebukes, the shame, and the transcendent glory of that opera. There followed a lifelong love of music, theater, and dance—the curtain opening on a stage of new discoveries.

Jeff Hawkins explains this exposure more scientifically as we make or feel an analogy between normally unrelated events:

> Creativity is mixing and matching patterns of everything you've ever experienced or come to know in your lifetime. The neural mechanism for doing this is everywhere in the cortex. . . . Everyone develops different models and memories of the world in his or her cortex and will make different analogies and predictions.

He cites exposure to music and later being able to play new instruments by making these "predictive leaps" built on the patterns in memory. But only when those experiences have been undertaken and stored. "Our predictions and thus our talents are built upon our experiences." (Hawkins and Blakeslee 2004 pp. 187–8).

References

CDC (Center for Disease Control) the National Youth Risk Behavior Study (YRBS), 2003.

Demers, Stephen; *Mind, Brain, Health & Education*, 2010, www.mbhe.org/movement.

Dwyer, Terence, James F. Sallis, Leigh Blizzard, Ross Lazarus, and Kimberlie Dean; *Relation of Academic Performance to Physical Activity and Fitness in Children* Pediatric Exercise Science, 13(3): 225–237, 2001.

Etnier, J.L., W. Salazar, D.M. Landers, S.J. Petruzzello, M. Han, and P. Nowell; *The Influence of Physical Fitness and Exercise upon Cognitive Functioning*: A Meta-Analysis, Journal of Sport & Exercise Psychology, September 1997

Hawkins, Jeff, and Sandra Blakeslee; *On Intelligence, Times Books*, New York: Henry Holt and Co., 2004.

Jenson, Eric; *Teaching with the Brain in Mind*, 2nd edition, ASCD, 2005. 2800 Shirlington Rd. Suite 1001, Arlington VA 22206

Jenson, Eric, and Liesl McConchie; *Brain-Based Learning: Teaching the Way Students Really Learn*, 3rd edition, Thousand Oaks: Corwin Press, Sage Publications, 2020.

Medina, John; *Brain Rules: 12 Rules for Surviving at Home, Work and School*, 2nd edition updated and expanded, Seattle: Pear Press, 2014, www.brainrules.com.

Mitchell, Debby; *Learning Through Movement and Music Assembled by Jean Blaydes*, www.humankinetics.com/products/all-products/Learning-through-Movement-and-Music.2012　*GeoMotion Group*

Ratey, J.M.D.; *Spark: The Revolutionary New Science of Exercise and the Brain*, Boston: Little, Brown and Company, 2008.

Sousa, David A.; *How the Brain Learns*, 5th edition, Thousand Oaks: Corwin Press, 2016.

7 The Developing Brain

This chapter concerning the developing brain is far removed from the subject of dynamic play and creative movement and I almost removed it. But as I thought about the astounding biological beginning that each of us—leaders and children—share, I thought it purposeful. If nature put so much into us, there must be a lot there still to use for whatever we choose to do with it. And if I am adding this section about an individual's beginning, how can I not include an equally thoughtful summary about the beginning of our species. Jeff Hawkins in his book *On Intelligence* (2004) describes the three epochs of its history. Added to this is commentary by Lisa Barrett in her book *Seven and a Half Lessons About the Brain* (2020).

Three Epochs of Evolution

Intelligence could be traced over three epochs, each using memory and prediction. The first would be when species used DNA as the medium for memory. Individuals could not learn and adapt within their lifetimes. They could only pass on the DNA-based memory of the world to their offspring through their genes. (Lisa Barrett, writing on this era of evolutionary learning, cites small creatures living on the ocean floor, amphioxi, who depended for nourishment on whatever approached, having no sensory mechanisms to branch out.)

The second epoch began when nature invented modifiable nervous systems that could quickly form memories. An individual could now learn about the structure of its

DOI: 10.4324/9781003254812-9

world and adapt its behavior accordingly within its lifetime. But an individual still could not communicate this knowledge to their offspring other than by direct observation. (Barrett colloquially describes the evolving of these more complicated sensory, motor, and nervous systems as posing one essential question: *is that thing in the distance good to eat or will it eat me?*)

The third and final epoch is unique to humans. It begins with the invention of language and the expansion of our large neocortex. We humans can learn a lot of the structure of the world within our lifetimes, and we can effectively communicate this to many other humans via language. You and I are participating in this process right now . . . We have become the most adaptable creatures on the planet and the only ones with the ability to transfer our knowledge of the world broadly within our populace. . . . The combination of a large neocortex and language has led to the spiraling success of our species.

(Hawkins and Blakeslee 2004 pp. 182–3)

The Brain in Embryo: Astounding Numbers

In less than one pound of gelatinous tissue, emotions, memories, dreams, and ideas are contained, evolving, and changing over a lifetime, wildly complex, even in a baby. Ten thousand nerve cells are contained in a single piece the size of a grain of rice. Each cell within that piece can make up to 10,000 neural connections.

Billions of brain cells forge links with billions of other cells, eventually making trillions of connections: trillions of crisscrossing wires. And all are following pathways, cues, and rules instructed by genetic codes. They *know* where to go. It is daunting to think how as parents or care providers we could possibly *use* all this opportunity provided by nature. We can't and are not intended to. It might be comforting to compare the situation to seeds dispersed into the air from the vegetation growing all around us. Nature consistently overprepares, ready for high winds or floods or drought, by sending countless seedlings into the air that go unplanted. About half of the 200 billion cells created in the first embryonic months of life die off by the 20th week of fetal life because they don't connect to what the body requires. So don't berate yourself for lost opportunities. Nature will overprepare in other ways to provide you with resources that are essential.

At four weeks of pregnancy, the first brain cells are forming—at the rate of 500,000 cells a minute. Some of those same cells will still function into old age if they are needed and used. The neurons forming at four weeks in embryo move along the neural tube which goes from the base of the spine to the brain. The neurons pass into the brain and grow layer by layer like an onion. The neurons travel in waves, millions every day, migrating down the neural tube, called the glia highway. They migrate to their destinations following cues along the way. Scientists don't know for sure how they know where to go, but they think the young migrating neurons, born from stem cells, take on the function of their neighbors traveling alongside them. What they believe is that the neurons have already received instruction when they begin their journey.

The neural connections that are used get strengthened; those that are not used become weak. The brain is constantly changing according to this use. The concept *use it or lose it* is a vital thesis of the brain throughout life. In other words, the brain develops itself: it grows depending on what it is experiencing.

It's hard to know what precisely influences fetal neural connections; however, we do know that the experiences of the pregnant mother in maintaining good nutrition and avoiding smoking and alcohol have effects on the developing fetus and on all of the developing cells in the brain and the body. Those experiences transfer directly to the baby.

At Birth: Billions of Brain Cells Ready and Able

Each person is born with more than 100 billion brain cells or neurons. Neural connections—the wires that enable brain cells to communicate with each other—continue forming in a new brain in breathtaking numbers and at unimaginable speeds The brain sends signals to thousands of other cells in the body at equally unimaginable speeds (DeBord 1998). At eight months, a baby's brain has about 1,000 trillion connections. These connections include synapses, the spaces between neurons across which the electrical signals that determine movement have to cross. Movement is powered by these electrical impulses sent out by the neurons. If a child wants to move his toe, a signal must go out from the neuron in his brain down to his toe. But it is not one long neuron that conducts that electrical signal; instead, it is a series of neurons that pass the electrical impulse along from one to another. Think of this process as a relay race. The electrical signal is passed like a baton from one neuron in the brain to the next one down the line to the next one after that and so on. Those spaces between these neurons, called synapses, are across which the electrical signal must jump. To help it make that jump, neurotransmitters are released that conduct the electrical signal from one neuron across the space to the receiving neuron.

Neurotransmitters are chemicals. They are excellent transmitters of electrical current, but scientists have discovered other distinctive ways in which neurotransmitters help the brain conduct its business—serotonin, dopamine, norepinephrine, and acetylcholine, to name a few. If these neurotransmitters are not available, the brain cannot function normally. For example, depression has been associated with problems associated with the neurotransmitter serotonin. Dopamine has been implicated in children who are diagnosed with attention-deficit/hyperactivity disorder (ADHD). Acetylcholine may be involved with the painful memories that lie behind cases of posttraumatic stress disorder (PTSD). In a child who is happy and well adjusted, these neurotransmitters are released and later reabsorbed in the spaces between the cells as needed to power movement and other necessary life processes. For example, norepinephrine incites the urge to take flight when danger is encountered.

All these connections begin declining so that at about age 10 about 500 trillion remain, continuing to decline relative to mental stimulation and the needs of the child to adapt to the environment he is born into. Experience of the outside world provides the stimulation, that is the input—the brain fuel that enters through the sensory systems—vision, hearing, smell, touch, and taste. In the first three years, foundations for thinking, language, vision, attitudes, and aptitudes are laid down. Between ages 4 and 12, the brain is exceedingly active, seeking information from the senses to determine what connections to keep and what to eliminate. Those not stimulated by the environment will be pruned. The window is open to age 12, as if to provide a big second chance (Kotulak 1996). A number of about 100 trillion connections is then what most can agree on. Learning, of course, continues afterward.

As these neural connections in the brain are made, new pathways form, and the capacity of the brain to make more connections increases. The brain grows itself. The more it is used, the more it expands; the less used, the more diminished it becomes. *Use it or lose it*; that notion persists throughout life.

In practical terms, providing early "brain food" might translate to providing stimulating experiences for the infant through sight, sound, and tactile experiences, input from the visual, auditory, and tactile senses to the neocortex. A parent might, for example, provide mobiles over the crib, colorful pictures within sight range, classical music, and touchable, movable objects. Ensuring comfort and contentment in the baby's bodily needs, such as involves feeding, burping, sleeping, changing diapers, and bathing, the baby does not have to center so intently on the problems of his innards and can focus outwardly on the wonders of his new world (Peck 2003). Multiple brain connections are made in every activity on which the child focuses. From birth onward, he is learning how to navigate a sea of changes and sensations, and in doing so, constructing a view of his world and the actions for how to live in it. We do this as adults; we create and modify a temperament and personality that can engage with life effectively.

Lisa Feldman Barrett in her provocative book *Seven and a Half Lessons about the Brain* explains for a layperson this complicated transmission of information going on continually, nonstop in the active brain: She describes the brain as a network of 128 billion neurons connected in a single, massive, and flexible structure, continually firing off communications to each other day and night. Electrical signals, when the neurons fire, race down the neuron's trunk to its roots, causing that to release chemicals (neurotransmitters) into the gaps between neurons—the synapses—"and voila" information is passed on, one neuron to another (Barrett 2020).

The Eye/Brain Connection

The brain has continued to develop in utero without visual experiences, but once vision begins, the connections are made like gangbusters. And they need to be made. Just one or two months of missing visual experiences can affect how the brain is wired and what it can do later on. A newborn baby's experience of sending images from the eye to the brain creates the connections the baby will be able to use throughout life. These connections—what the eye sees and processes through the visual cortex—are what stimulate the brain to create the wiring it will use: to think, choose, feel emotion, create, and so on.

Jeff Hawkins and Blakeslee (2004) probe the neocortex and explain how input originating in the retina of both eyes is relayed through the visual regions of the brain in split-second, changing patterns to ultimate recognition of an object. This brain activity is continuous throughout our lives.

Vision is the last of the senses to develop; nevertheless, by two days of age, a baby can recognize by sight alone, the mother. This is so, although neither the eye nor the brain is fully developed. What the baby sees is comparable to a faded photograph seen through a tube.

The baby follows moving shapes; she has a remarkable ability to cut out bothersome, overstimulating lights and sounds to focus on those shapes. Moving shapes like those displayed in a mobile, exercise her eye/brain activity and promote active neural connections. So too does the visual attention paid to her, as parents and others make eye contact.

The Nature–Nurture Deliberation

The question of whether nature or nature prevails in children's development is still asked, but being able to see inside the brain adds evidence that both are determinate. The brain has remarkable plasticity and continually uses both experience and environment to shape it. It does this throughout life, making connections, tuning to adapt, and pruning to discard connections that are not used.

Genetics plays a part—experience is not etched upon a blank slate—but adding a stimulating environment builds on the genetic structure that is inherited. Experience in the outside environment refines the circuitry of the brain; this influences which connections are stabilized. Those stabilized connections remaining secure in the brain's memory cause it to make predictions for future actions, "intelligent" actions based on past experiences.

Utilizing the enormous flexibility of the brain, nature and nurture together change the brain's structure and performance. The caretaker's task is to maintain the connections made and stimulate new ones. The following passage, written by Dan Cloer about synaptic connections, clarifies the structure, relationship, and impact between neurons *genetically* provided, and synaptic connections created by *experience*. Touched on earlier in this chapter, perhaps these all-important lifelong connections will be better understood:

> Within the brains of all animals and humans, continuous interactions and chemical communications occur between cells called neurons. These cells have the appearance of long fibers with fingerlike projections at both ends. At one end, the fingers serve as antennae, at the other end as transmitters. Neurons do not physically touch each other. The spaces between the transmitters of one and the antennae of another are called synapses. The receipt of a messenger molecule (neurotransmitter) at the antenna triggers a sequence of cellular activity that results in another messenger molecule being transmitted from the opposite end of the cell. These molecules

cross the synapse to the next antenna, and so it goes, like a wave of dominoes. Messenger molecules are degraded or reabsorbed, and the neuron is again at rest, ready for the next wave.

(Vision June 2004)

Many thousands of neurons may be interconnected through these fingers, not only in series but also in a mass of branching networks. Each cell becomes a hub, with spokes leading to other areas of the brain. While the physical alignment of neural cells is presently seen as being determined genetically, the synaptic connections between cells are malleable and constantly changing. Our experiences determine the functioning of these neural connections and the predictive operation of the brain. During a lifetime of experiences, synaptic connections are continually made and unmade, forming a vast, ever-changing neural network. The brain is different today than it was yesterday. As the brain provides the physical substrate of mind, we can therefore say that, at some level, our minds are constantly changing.

Coming to understand the synaptic processes that gather, store, and retrieve information throughout the brain is the cutting edge of modern neuroscience. The impact of learning through experience is being shown to be more important than evolutionary psychology's concept of innate determinism. The study of psychology has changed with the profound advances in the science of the brain.

The Flexibility of a Child's Brain

A younger brain has more flexibility to change than an older brain. The brain's plasticity makes it capable of infinite modification and expansion; it is perfectly designed for learning. How fortunate that is, for there is so much to learn, and this learning must take place expediently too. It is said that the human infant takes the longest of any species to survive on its own.

The flexibility of the baby's brain is demonstrated in the baby's limitless capacity to absorb sounds and organize sounds into categories. Experiments recording brain activity in babies up to 11 months demonstrate that babies have the ability to hear and distinguish minute differentiation in sounds, more so than adults. Because of this, different languages can be learned more easily at an early age and the sounds between them differentiated more efficiently. What occurs, however, is that the baby becomes a specialist in one language, the native one. The baby then begins to listen through that filter, which is mapping out the sounds being mastered.

Language

A system of neurons generates language. We may hear physically through our ears, but we hear mentally through our brains. Learning language provides leaps of brain connectivity in which we learn from the experience of others, not just our own. Learning depends on different systems in the brain to process such intricacies as syllables and sounds. The neural patterns the brain must discern to process language, let alone meaning, are formidable.

As babies hear, they simultaneously organize the sounds, placing them in categories and after about 11 months, they ignore the distinctions that do not serve the native language being used. In the ensuing months, the brain becomes ever more complex in allowing the baby to organize and categorize not only the sounds and syllables but also the meanings.

Story Reading

Reading is a complex performance of the brain. Many aspects of the brain are being used as a story is told or read: there is letter naming, letter perception, word perception, syntax, the assimilation of vocabulary, and concepts of recognition and comprehension. Children learn to put hundreds of concepts together when they learn to read.

Reading has to be explicitly taught for the sound of the words and the visual image on the page to come together. Then after seeing the visual image and ascertaining how the words sound, the reader must use judgment to put it all together so that it makes sense. Even a single letter sets off a complex series of reactions in the brain:

1. The brain focuses attention on the reading task.
2. The brain captures a visual representation of the letter.
3. The brain sends this to a special area of the brain where the visual symbol gets hooked up to the letter's sound and meaning.
4. The letter is articulated.

Conclusion

Brain development never stops, even though large sections remain permanent. This is because the brain adapts to the world it encounters with flexibility. In this adaptation, it encodes in its circuits our memories, hopes, aspirations, who we love, and who we disdain. The brain is an ideal mechanism for learning because of its remarkable plasticity. The impossible part has been done for us; nature has made it so. We add nurture and the whole child, in body, mind, and spirit, is on its way.

In early childhood, neural connectivity is greatest. In adolescence, another great surge occurs, which may account for some of the problems connected with adolescent rebellion (and teenage weirdness). But when a foundation is built earlier, such as interest in the arts or sports or academics, or one has attained the self-confidence and interest in the world to want to fly to the moon (metaphorically), that second surge of neural energy at adolescence will have a natural boost. From there it can lift off into mature achievement. The unfortunate reverse is sometimes the case: a painful plummet when surging adolescent energies have no targets in sight. The problems arising then require sensitive mitigation. How much less costly and more effective would have been the music lessons early on.

We know now that not only do we not lose brain cells, as once was thought, but they continue to grow throughout life, even into maturity. When they are used. Thus, as aging adults, to remain intellectually active, curious, and creative is to provide fuel for our faithful old brains.

The brain controls and regulates all our internal organs. What if we had to program our heartbeats, push buttons to digest our food, pull strings to lift our arms and bend our joints? So involved with our functions we would be, we could do little else, like hold a job or play or love or create. Well, the brain just as mysteriously performs functions we do not see but feel and intuit: our understanding, emotions, creativity, and sensitivities (Dowling 1998). It is profoundly beautiful to sense this amazing technology within us. To use or to lose. Because that's the deal we are offered.

References

Barrett, Lisa Feldman; *Seven and a Half Lessons About the Brain*, Boston and New York: Houghton Mifflin Harcourt, 2020.

Cloer, Daniel; Vision Magazine, June 2004, https://www.vision.org/.

DeBord, Karen, January 13, 1998, www.nncc.org/Child.Dev/brain-nc.html.

Dowling, John E.; *Creating Mind*, New York and London: W.W. Norton, 1998.

Hawkins, Jeff, and Sandra Blakeslee; *On Intelligence, Times Books*, New York: Henry Holt and Co., 2004.

Kotulak, Ronald; *Inside the Brain: Revolutionary Discoveries of How the Mind Works*, Kansas City, MO: Andrews McMeel Publishing Co., 1996 (pgs. xiv, xv, 5,6,7, 34–45).

Peck, Judith; *Smart Starts in the Arts*, Mahwah: Imagination Arts Publications, 2003.

8 The Brain, Movement, and Dance

I love all the muscles, I love all the joints, I love all the spatial dimensions, I love all the possible relationships.
—Irene Dowd's delightful exclamation, excerpted from *Teacher's Wisdom* in *Dance Magazine* (2005).

Any child could have said this, were they to put words to their love of catapulting through space.

Moving with Intention

Some educators use the phrase "Movement with Intention" in expressing the value of physical movement to enhance brain activity This occurs with engagement in the projects and stories involved in learning through dynamic play. A 2011 study by the American Academy of Pediatrics shows that intentional movement can improve test scores. There is growing evidence that this kind of exercise is good not only for the body but also for the mind. Projects in dynamic play can help this along by suggesting some lively "intentions." The factor of play itself is important in children's learning, advocated in an AAP Journal article (Milteer et al. 2012).

> Play is essential to the social, emotional, cognitive, and physical well-being of children beginning in early childhood. It is a natural tool for children to develop resiliency as they learn to cooperate, overcome challenges, and negotiate with others. Play also allows children to be creative. It provides time for parents to be fully engaged with

DOI: 10.4324/9781003254812-10

their children, to bond with their children, and to see the world from the perspective of their child. However, children who live in poverty often face socioeconomic obstacles that impede their rights to have playtime, thus affecting their healthy social-emotional development. For children who are under-resourced to reach their highest potential, it is essential that parents, educators, and pediatricians recognize the importance of lifelong benefits that children gain from play. (Milteer et al. 2012).

Dance involves a greater range of motion, strength, and endurance than most other physical activities. This is accomplished through movement patterns that promote coordination and kinesthetic memory. Utilizing the entire body, dance is a form of exercise for total body fitness. Of course, young children are naturally active, but dance offers an avenue to expand movement possibilities and skills. Agility, balance, flexibility, these are attributes that serve ordinary mobility, enhanced when dance is added to the routine of everyday life.

Getting Inside the Body

Peter Lovatt in his study of the science of dance, *The Dance Cure* (2021) explains the effectiveness of intentional movement and its physical attributes:

> When we move and start to get our hearts pumping, we set off a complex chain of biological events, which can fundamentally change the way we think and solve problems. The first thing that happens is an increase in the rate at which blood is pumped around our body. This is important because a lot of this blood, between 15 and 20% of it, goes to the brain. This is vital, because brain cells will die without the oxygen that the blood carries to them. Blood is like a freight train, transporting things into and out of the brain. In addition to oxygen, it carries carbohydrates, amino acids, fats, hormones and vitamins into the brain and carbon dioxide, ammonia, lactate and hormones away from it.

(p. 73)

But Lovatt goes further, carrying this physical vitality into other realms of the human condition:

> Dancing stimulates the link between the body and brain; in fact, it provides a full brain and body massage! Signals are relayed from the motor area of the brain to nerves, muscles and joints, and the moving body also sends signals back to different parts of the brain and creates activity both deep down at the core of the nervous system and in the neocortex, the brain's outer layer.
>
> (p. 69)

Dance and Learning

Beyond the extensive physical attributes, dance affords are the notable rewards for the whole person. The National Dance Education Organization on its website www.ndeo. org/ maintains:

> Dance contributes to students' physical, emotional, and social well-being by providing a method of physical awareness and fitness, an outlet for creativity and personal expression, and a means to develop social-emotional skills, such as self-management, relationship skills, and responsible decision-making. Students who study dance develop 21st century skills such as collaboration, communication, and creativity, and dance has been shown to positively affect students' attitudes, perceptions, and values. Dance provides children multiple perspectives. Through dance, children develop enhanced sensory awareness, cognition, and consciousness. It is this heightened state that creates the magic of movement that is dance.

Peter Lovatt expands on the connection between dance and problem-solving, dance and learning, explaining that the dynamic brain is where we do our thinking, and its effective functioning relies on a variety of molecular, vascular, and cellular structures. The intentional movement found in dance increases the production of proteins and the neurotransmitters of dopamine and serotonin, the latter chemical boosting mood and behavior which can promote a positive attitude toward learning. Other salient factors in the brain–body connection are also at work.

Dancing is different from standard aerobic exercises, such as pedaling away on an exercise bike or running on a treadmill. When we dance, we also stimulate those areas of the brain responsible for a range of mental activities such as spatial awareness, memory, perception, learning, and interpersonal cooperation. It is the stimulation of this complex and intricate, interconnected network that underpins the extraordinary link between moving and super-sharp thinking.

Research teams around the world have been studying the links between movement, neurocognitive function, and creativity for decades and have made some astonishing findings. What's more, these findings can be applied easily in our everyday lives (Lovatt 2021 p. 69–74).

Teachers would be wise to alternate periods of their young students sitting at desks and focusing on the curricular lesson plan with improvisational creative movement. Not only is this an opportunity to sharpen thinking, as Lovatt and others argue, but it provides an opportunity for children who for one reason or another are not keeping up with the academics to be on a par with others. Reasons for lagging behind the lessons, in many instances, involve problems in the home environment of which the teacher is unaware. In group discussions preceding the creative movement improvisations, these children can leave behind their unexpressed struggles to focus on school lessons and, instead, with their verbal and physical contributions accepted, feel equally capable. The section on self-esteem that follows later in this chapter suggests how enhancing this notion of capability can lead to better focus on those school lessons as well.

Learning and Imagination

Taking the argument of the relationship between movement and learning further while adding the cognitive elements that dance provides, let's add *imagination* to the mix and factor the notion of creativity into learning. Guy Claxton in his book *Intelligence in the Flesh* argues strongly for blending creativity into learning to increase its breadth and depth. He cites as an example of the effectiveness of that relationship, the experimental way in which artists and artisans approach the regularly occurring problems in their work. These problems are often seen as opportunities to make new discoveries. Tinkering and experimenting spark imagination and branching out beyond the controlled reasoning that houses what you already know: "Imagination, like emotion, is a halfway house between body and mind." By this he means feeling or sensing in your body what is progressing in your mind and acting on it.

He argues that reasoning is not senior to other ways of learning but should blend into them. Purely intellectual learning, as done in many schools, can become dull, as compared with hands-on methods allowing the learner to use "the whole gamut of learning methods woven together . . . looking carefully and feeling with their fingers . . . imagining and wondering about new possibilities; and being thoughtful and self-critical too." He argues for recognizing the restricted modes of intelligence we often operate under, "identified with the particular verbal and quantitative measures of the schoolhouse and IQ tests" and recognizing the intelligence of the body in its multifarious processes (Claxton 2015 pp. 238–241).

It is interesting if not astounding to know that imagining something—that is, putting yourself virtually in a place or situation—acts in your brain as an experience. This happens because the brain picks it up and uses it to form its patterns for prediction of your next decisions and actions. "Your brain functions in patterns," explains Jeff Hawkins, "coalescing sights, sound and touch." All the senses involved in creating experience. He presents the example of petting a dog and the different aspects of experience that involves: seeing, hearing, petting, and processing that information. This is electrical activity firing in patterns, all streaming in on the input axons of neurons. (Hawkins 2004)

So as you employ imagination to blend with your reasoning skills and the intake of your senses and the signals your body sends—the complete arsenal of your learning apparatus—more than learning occurs; you are creating intelligence. Here is an example excerpted and shortened from *Smart Starts in the Arts: Fostering Intelligence, Creativity and Serenity in the Early Years*, my book for parents and childcare providers. The context is imaginative problem-solving that accomplishes effective learning along with the pleasant experience of shared play, as opposed to discipline that doesn't go anywhere:

> MaryAnne's room is a mess and as the parent in charge you ask the child to put away her toys strewn all over the floor. You are teaching good habits, besides limiting back-bending and risk of a broken ankle. But other than your asking she has no reason to straighten the room. She sees no mess, only coveted possessions awaiting her pleasure. Straightening the room would be a rote action of complying to your demand (good enough you might well argue) but as will be shown a shallow success in learning—doing something without a reason—and a missed opportunity all around. The solution offered is that Mr. and Mrs. Wigglebottom are coming to dinner in half an hour and the party is being held in this very room. Dinner is to be prepared on her own toy stove and served on her own toy dishes. But Holy Moley, look at this room! In the imaginary scene into which she is propelled, she becomes aware of space—where would they sit?—of movements, the visiting couple knocking over fragile spires of Lego blocks, stuffed tigers, bears, an elephant and unnamed others. Fun images then might appear of serving tea to her hungry menagerie. She nods dramatically as you leave, brows furrowed. Indeed, when you appear 10 minutes later with a purse in one hand and leading Mr. Wigglebottom with the other, the room is straightened. You stop to praise the lovely appearance of everything, the fancy dishes and the tiny table and

chairs all set up. The nibbling of cookies and cheerful conversation between Mrs. Wigglebottom and two dolls who have joined the table only adds to the joyous event.

(Peck 2003 pp. 59–60)

Although this describes imaginative learning with a young child, the concept works with older children—or, for that matter, adults—asking that something be seen in the mind's eye. "Please feed the dog; he's hungry," you plead. But you fail to succeed, for there is something to be done elsewhere or the couch and TV hold sway with inertia as their companion. But conveying, with some theatrical performance perhaps, being hungry, running home from school in anticipation of graham crackers and milk, or being stuck in car traffic picturing dinner on the table. These remembrances of hunger can evoke a visceral urgency to feed the dog. *Picturing* such as this—putting yourself in another's place—are what gives rise to empathy, that state in which we are most human. Most important, there arises, in these portrayals, a genuine reason to do the errand, not someone else's but your own.

The Body's Role in Emotional Well-Being

Can You Choose to Be Happy? And Can the Body Help?

The ability to make negative situations positive is something that can be learned. Existing neural pathways to do this can be strengthened with exercise using the brain's plasticity. You can choose to be happy. James Hamblin, in *If Our Bodies Could Talk* (2016), applauds Mary Kay Morrison, sitting president of the Association for Applied and Therapeutic Humor whose work uses humor to increase positive associations in the brain. The results are that laughter releases endorphins, like running or consuming opium. Hamblin writes that laughter decreases the stress hormones cortisol and epinephrine, thereby improving the function of the immune system. It works even if you just feign laughter. The very act of laughter even devoid of humor seems to have positive effects on blood pressure and mood (Hamblin 2016).

You can choose to find humor in unsatisfactory or deadening situations. You can choose to be happy. This surely is a positive thought.

Music, the feel of it, like laughter if dancing accompanies it, can produce a sensation of joy. Or at the very least shake negative feelings, suggests Dr. Lovatt in *The Dancing Cure*. The aspect of exercise in dancing, along with the emotional response to whatever music is involved, releases dopamine in different parts of the brain that brings on that happy feeling. Studies show that even short periods of dance—30 minutes— were successful in reducing depression and increasing vitality, while other similar studies showed increased relaxation and reduction of stress hormones.

Yet, it seems we don't customarily let our emotions freely show. We muffle them. How many times on television have we seen a person interviewed about the death of a close relative emit a soft laugh while telling about it instead of the blood-curdling howl she must feel? "Most of our lives are spent disconnecting our emotions from our physical expression of them," writes Dr. Lovatt. "Unless you're a six-year-old or a Labrador, you cannot freely and spontaneously express yourself." But then, he suggests, "Dancing gives humans a tail to wag" (Lovatt 2021 p. 116).

The Purpose of Emotion

Emotions give shape and direction to whatever we do. The word comes from the Latin *emovere*, which means "to move out." Bessel van der Kolk in his book *The Body Keeps the Score* cites Darwin's intensive research on emotion when late in life he published *The Expression of the Emotions in Man and Animals*. Darwin concluded that the fundamental purpose of emotion is to initiate movement, actions especially for safety and physical equilibrium. We don't think of emotion as a precursor to movement, as so often intense emotions lay us so low we can't move at all. But emotions are intimately tied to the body, its gut and heart, and if overused or prolonged, they can become stuck in survival mode, which is to avoid danger—stay out of its way. This stultified place is no place for happiness to reign. There, energies cannot focus on the positive, outgoing realms of love, bonding, learning, and other people's needs. States van der Kolk, "Heart, guts and brain communicate intimately via the pneumogastric nerves involved in the expression and management of emotions in both humans and animals. Under intense emotion, feeling the pain viscerally in our gut, we want desperately to make it go away."

The Intensity of Emotion

Dr. van der Kolk speaks of social relationships being front and center in the understanding of trauma and healing as well. "When the message we receive from another person is 'You're safe with me,' we relax. Warm accepting relationships can make us feel nourished, supported and restored." In dynamic play during the group's verbal engagement preceding their improvisations when children share their ideas, there seems a relaxation of tension in the ease with which thoughts are thrown into the ring. It may be the release of stress that transports their energies into the creative expression that follows. A teacher customarily has no easy access to what goes on in children's home life or what transpires socially with classmates at school. Yet these issues can take center stage in a child's school performance. Being able to feel safe with other people is probably the single most important aspect of mental health according to van der Kolk's extensive research; safe connections are fundamental to meaningful and satisfying lives, with the critical issue being reciprocity, being heard and seen by those around us.

The last thing that should be cut from school schedules," he argues, "are chorus, physical education, recess, and anything else involving movement, play and joyful engagement." It is of ultimate importance to engage the "safety systems" of the brain to make children emotionally receptive to new ideas rather than total concentration on recruiting the cognitive capacities of the mind (van der Kolk 2014 pp. 75–86). So getting back to Darwin and appreciating his insights on how we evolved, might help us to evolve better, understanding that the purpose of emotions is to initiate movement and action. We might then value its intensity for all the positive vitality it provides.

Brain and Self-Esteem

By the time we are adults, married and perhaps parents, we have amassed an arsenal of defense systems against hurt. We strike out to blame the perceived attacker or withdraw or walk away or employ one of the vast number of compensatory mechanisms we've acquired through the years. With these moves, we preserve the fragile shell of self-esteem which shelters the confidence and dignity we require to meet the abrasive demands of living.

But children have garnered no such acquired protection. Although nature has fortified their developing personalities with a magnificent resilience, which serves to keep them swinging, so to say, repeated abuse and the hurt that follows can break that down.

> A child who has been ignored or chronically humiliated is likely to lack self-respect. Children who have not been allowed to assert themselves will probably have difficulty standing up for themselves as adults, and most grown-ups who were brutalized as children carry a smoldering rage that will take a great deal of energy to contain.
>
> (van der Kolk 2014 pp. 304–5)

An arsenal of defense systems is built, some quite nasty, even the normal ones. These need to be understood, unpretty as they are, especially those formed when abuse has firmly fastened itself inside that fragile shell that harbors self-esteem. The behaviors need not be erased but modified for positive, even productive use. Like the fictional but valiant Superman, there exists in the human psyche such a hero to come to the rescue. It is the very brain we hold inside whose mission is dedicated to our survival.

The brain can take command of those three endowments I stated earlier, possessed by children and so well utilized in learning, and direct them to engage. Where better than to place physical energy, imagination, and the need for self-expression than in such vigorous efforts as sports or the arts—music, fine art, drama, or dance—where they can eloquently be put to use?

Children's resilience allows for this, as does the presence of each of those three natural energies. But it is the caretaker's job to bring these worthy outlets onto the scene with exposure and ease of access. Such exposure is essential, especially where self-esteem is wanting. "Anticipating rejection, ridicule, and deprivation, [children] are reluctant to try out new options, certain that these will lead to failure," states van der Kolk. Nevertheless, researchers and we ourselves can cite examples proving that the effort pays back well, particularly in the adolescent years when hormones and natural efforts at independence create their ubiquitous challenges. Having a standing accomplishment at the ready to contain all that energy is key.

The group interactions during dynamic play, it bears repeating, create a format for the bolstering of self-esteem, as a child's verbalized ideas and responses to the ideas of others receive acceptance. Van der Kolk in a nutshell: "The critical issue is reciprocity, being heard and seen by those around us."

Brain Activity and the Arts in General

Research has been ongoing and intensive about the positive effects of the arts, including dance and music, to active brain growth and stimulation.

Michael I. Poser Ph.D. and Brenda Patoine in their research relating the brain to study of the arts—music, dance, drama and/or visual art—find a correlation with the attention networks of the brain that can improve cognition generally.

They write: "We know that the brain has a system of neural pathways dedicated to attention. We know that training these attention networks improves general measures of intelligence." The result of their research argues strongly that more attention be paid to the arts in education (Poser and Patoine 2009).

Dr. Bruce Perry (and the CIVITAS Healing Arts project) state:

> . . . research has shown that specific parts of the brain are stimulated by specific artistic enrichment modalities. For example: the base or brain stem responds to touch; the midbrain to music-making and movement; the limbic region to dance, art, play therapy, and nature discovery; and the cortical region to art, storytelling, drama, and writing. Through artistic stimulation, children's brains are healing and growing.
>
> Duggal Visual Solutions (Feb. 11, 2015)

Figure 8.1 Moving with intention. Three boys explore conflict and camaraderie through movement.

Source: Courtesy of CityStep.

Van der Kolk writes: "The capacity of art, music, and dance to circumvent the speechlessness that comes with terror may be one reason they are used as trauma treatments in cultures around the world."

Play involving physical movement, which most play does, is shown to increase cognition. Dance has multiple added features in this regard. Jenny Seham of the National Dance Institute documents measurable academic and social results for school children who study dance. She specifically notes "positive changes in self-discipline, grades, and sense of purpose in life" that her students demonstrate.

("Dance Partners: A Model of Inclusive Arts Education," in S.M. Malley [Ed.], *Exemplary Programs and Approaches*, pp. 80–100).

The literature on the overall value of the arts in education is vast and well understood. It is also readily available and needs no further references in this text.

References

Claxton, Guy; *Intelligence in the Flesh*, New Haven and London: Yale University Press, 2015.

Dowd, Irene; *Teacher's Wisdom*, Dance Magazine, June 2005.

Hamblin, J.M.D.; *If Our Bodies Could Talk*, New York: Doubleday, 2016.

Hawkins, Jeff, and Sandra Blakeslee; *On Intelligence*, New York: Times Books, Henry Holt, 2004.

Lovatt, Peter; *The Dance Cure*, New York: Harper Collins, 2021.

Milteer, Regina M., Kenneth R. Ginsburg, Council on Communications and Media Committee on Psychosocial Aspects of Child and Family Health, Deborah Ann Mulligan, and Nusheen Ameenuddin; *The Importance of Play in Promoting Healthy Child Development and Maintaining Strong Parent-Child Bond: Focus on Children in Poverty*, Pediatrics, 129(1):e204–e213, January 2012.

The National Dance Education Organization, www.ndeo.org/.

Peck, Judith; *Smart Starts in the Arts*, Mahwah: Imagination Arts Publications, 2003.

Perry, Bruce; *The CIVITAS Healing Arts Project*, Duggal Visual Solutions, Feb. 11, 2015, https://www.bdperry.com/about.

Poser, Michael I., and Brenda Patoine *How Arts Training Improves Attention and Cognition. Cerebrum, 2-4. https://www.researchgate. net/ (Sept. 2009).*

Van der Kolk, Bessel.M.D.; *The Body Keeps the Score*, New York: Viking, 2014.

Part III

The Creative Conquest of Space

Figure 9.0 The sense of freedom in self-expression comes not from wanting to fly but the feeling that you can.

Credit line: Courtesy of Alice Teirstein.

DOI: 10.4324/9781003254812-11

Part III
The Creative Conquest
of Space

9   Taking Off

Transforming Shape into Movement

A child's normal vocabulary of movement usually includes walking, running, hopping, skipping, bending, crouching, reaching, waving, and so forth. These activities, if expanded and exaggerated can become expressive movements. But to provide children with a physical vocabulary equal to the voice of their imagination, other movements must be added to this: Movements with shape. The shapes are all around you. You move in and around them, touch and bump into them. These are shapes your body can emulate: round, straight, curved, twisted, flexed, stretched, contracted, released, expanded, and elevated.

Transforming these shapes into movement is unfamiliar, not difficult, and easier than skipping when first attempted. The shapes become kinesthetic when transferred to expressive movements, for example, hovering, soaring, hiding, or emerging.

With the development of a rich physical vocabulary, children can be both original in their improvisations and honest in their expressions: original because an endless variety of interesting movements can be created; honest because cliche patterns are not copied. How many times have you seen children interpret an elephant by bending over and swinging clasped hands from side to side? Have you ever seen a child interpret an elephant in a different manner? Certainly there is more to an elephant than his trunk! Every time a child is given this assignment, natural abilities are restrained in favor of the cliche; the child becomes more adept at copying than

DOI: 10.4324/9781003254812-12

at discovering. Instead, when encouraged to think about the elephant's size and heavy weight and wrinkled texture and slow gait, images begin to form in the child's mind, and it is a short and eager trip from there to the body.

The Dance of the Butterfly

The following example may be helpful in understanding why acquiring a vocabulary of movement is so important. When children, unfamiliar with creative movement, are asked to interpret a butterfly, they usually run in a circle flapping their arms up and down. They are, in effect, presenting a stereotyped impression of a butterfly without visualizing one themselves. It is the only way they know but neither original nor honest and cannot be called creative. The butterfly image is more profitably explored if the leader and the group discuss the butterfly first by visualizing its colors and patterns, its way of alighting on a flower, how it folds its wings and spreads them. Then the butterfly can be physically interpreted in a group. High and low movements can be contrasted to indicate the motion of the butterfly in space. Changing head directions and arm patterns in place can express the bright and varied colors. The leader, by verbal and physical suggestion, helps the children probe their own impressions of the style and singular beauty of a butterfly. Bringing in colorful illustrations is always helpful in the discussion.

Forming a Mental Image

Seeing
Feeling
Thinking
Speaking

It is not necessary for you, the leader, to be adept at moving to accomplish the probing of a mental image. You need only focus on what is being portrayed and trust the validity of your own mental image of the object, animal, issue, emotion, or

Figure 9.1 With a rich physical vocabulary children can be both original and honest in their expressions, producing images from their inner eye.

Credit line: Courtesy of Alice Teirstein.

situation being considered. Seeing or feeling the thing to be interpreted is half the battle won. It then becomes easy to relate it to physical terms.

The children must also be encouraged to see with their own eyes and to verbalize their impressions. When they become aware that their personal aesthetic judgments are valued by the group, they are eager to develop those ideas further. *Confidence in the validity of their own judgment* is not only an essential ingredient in creative expression it can affect children's aptitude for decision-making in general.

Formations

The projects are best done by arranging participants in one of three basic formations:

1. Wide circle—for narrow movements in place
2. Middle of the room—spread out for broad spatial movements and for projects done with partners or in groups
3. Single-line formation —Lined up to move singly or two by two from corner to corner of the room—for runs, leaps, and skips across the floor

Wide Circle and Middle of the Room Formations

A circle formation tends to create an informal group atmosphere. Also, children gain confidence and inspiration by watching others move around them. In addition, the leader can easily give encouragement to anyone in the circle by a simple nod of praise. Create a wide circle by having everyone join hands in a ring, then drop hands, and take three "giant" steps back. If the room is not large enough for the children to make a good circle, children should form lines, arm's distance apart, facing the leader. Suggest working in pairs, which can stimulate creative movement by repeating a partner's movement and expanding on it.

Use your judgment when to use a circle formation or the middle of the room. Young children are not overly self-conscience about their movements, while older children are hesitant about others seeing their movements at such close

Figure 9.2 Pairs communicate with each other through movement, putting their expressivity into hands and fingers as well as bodies. Here, they work in partners in a circle formation.

Source: Courtesy of CityStep.

range. The type of formation to use will also depend as well on the size of the group and the space available.

Single-Line Formations

The single-line formation should be used for broad movements across the floor. Such movements require the full length of the room. To allow each child enough expanse, children form a line in one corner of the room. The line is set with one child at a time moving or two together depending on the width of the room, the size of the group, and the amount of time at your disposal. Each set moves across the floor before the next set starts out. When the children arrive at the opposite corner, they keep their formation and repeat the movement returning across the floor.

10 Ground Instruments

This chapter is geared towards students amassing the physical vocabulary that will produce movements that can be both expressive and honest. Elements of contrast are fun to do with partners or in small groups. At the end of the chapter, a list is provided as a reference for the leader to help organize the sessions, starting with movements in the middle of the room and, after warm-up, the more expansive moves across the floor.

Legs and Feet

Trees: Look out the window and study a tree. The trunk of the tree is strong and tall. Maintain your balance while slowly swaying like the tree might in a strong wind. The tree *swaaaaays* but stays upright because of its long, thick roots.

Brooms: Begin with feet together. Always alternate legs so that one does not work more than the other. Like powerful brooms sweeping the floor, swing your legs forward and backward, one at a time, toes extended. Do this at first with straight legs like Snow White's broom sweeping the floor of the Seven Dwarves' home. Then do the swings with a bent leg as if "Dopey" has taken the broom to sweep. Next swing across the body and back on a diagonal, first straight and then like "Dopey." You can hold onto a chair if you need to. Finally, swing across and to the side with each leg adding a step in between, and you can "sweep" right across the floor.

DOI: 10.4324/9781003254812-13

Cross-side step; cross-side step, sweeping all across the room. Swing your arms to help keep your balance.

Muscles: When you want to hold your leg in the air, you can command it to stay. Tell your muscles silently, just by thinking about it, what it is you want them to do. Try this for a few minutes; then do the leg swings as you did in "Brooms." But when the leader says, "Hold!" think, "Hold," which is telling your leg to stay up. Repeat the swings and the holds whenever you want and praise your obedient muscles for doing everything you tell them to.

Fun with obedient muscles: Move around the room then stop to silently tell your muscles to kick your leg high in front. And then to the side. And then any which way. Give both legs a chance to show you what they can do. Holding onto a chair show how in command you are of your muscles, holding them straight or bent. Swing them and see how fast your muscles get the message to change direction. Now add your arms and torso and show how muscles all over your body will hold you in as many different positions as you choose. What power you have. Go for it. (This project can be followed by showing anatomic drawings of muscle attachment to bone and by a simple explanation of how muscles work.)

Shoes: Try on different kinds of shoes. Here are some examples, but you can find many more:

- Ballet shoes: Lace imaginary ballet shoes on your feet and dance. Dance all around the room turning from time to time and sometimes leaping. Then, standing still, lift your chest, pull in your tummy, and try to balance on one leg. Lift your other leg just for a moment; then dance some more. How long can you balance each time? How high can you lift your leg?

- Firefighting boots: Trudge through the wet building hauling the heavy hose. Search the corners and wave away anyone you see to clear away, out of danger.

- Skates: Glide and spin, using your arms for balance. Race with your arms behind you against the wind.

Skate backward glancing over your shoulder. Skate with a partner.

- Seven-league boots: Leap a mile with each step.
- Skis: How your body twists, knees one way, arms the other way. Down you ski, dodging a bush, skirting around a tree.
- Stocking feet: Quietly, softly, nobody hears you. All around the house you can go while nobody hears. Open the fridge and take an apple. Munch it while you go. Quietly, softly, almost skating at times, tip-toeing at others.
- Cat's paws: Lightly jump up (like onto a table), lightly bound (like after a mouse), lightly step up to your dish of food, so picky.
- Underwater flappers: Swim long distances. Weave over and under the waves; your flippers propel you like a fish.

Jumps: With feet together bend your knees and spring off the floor. Land in the starting position with knees bent. An imaginary spring hidden in the ball of your foot makes you spring like a jack-in-the-box. Pressing down it gets ready and—released!—sends you high in the air. Better have somebody set a pillow on the head of everyone following you to prevent the ceiling from cracking if they jump too high. (For a laugh, the leader instructs the children to stay in the air until told to come down and then scolds them for disobeying. An adjunct to the project is a brief study of gravity.) Remember: all jumps begin and end with bent legs even though the spring in the air is straight and strong. A few other improvisational jumps are bouncing balls, kangaroos, rabbits, and jumping beans. For variation, jump in half turns and full turns and jump to rhythmic beats of a drum.

Leaping over puddles: With an imaginary umbrella, the leader looks around, dismayed by all the puddles the rain has left. You need to leap over every one of them.

There's water underneath. So if you fall in the water, you get wet!

Pony trots: With your knees bent, toes pointed, and arms out in front, trot like a show pony across the room. Keep your chest high and back straight and try to make your trot as smooth as possible.

Circus ponies: Do the pony trots this time with elevation. With each trot spring high in the air off the ball of your foot.

Racehorse: Now the pony has no time for fancy trotting. This horse's rider needs to win. Leap across the room making the longest strides you can. When the race is over, how about creating a horse show: Alternate circus pony trots (high and bouncy—adding a turn or two) with racehorse leaps (long and low), contrasting the two.

Figure 10.1 Like a racehorse you leap across the room, others cheering you on.

Credit line: Courtesy of Alice Teirstein.

Skips: Skip across the room but add some variations:

- A gay and lively skip, tossing your head from side to side
- A high, springy skip, bouncing off the ball of your foot
- A combination of run, run, skip repeated across the floor trying to get as *high* as you can in the skip
- A skip in circles

Figure 10.2 Improvisational skips. Skip, thinking of ideas and emotions—happiness, excitement, or wondering what's around the corner.

Credit line: Courtesy of Alice Teirstein.

- Skips changing directions, first one way and then another
- Skips in ways that suggest ideas or feelings: feeling bold, being cautious, feeling happy, tired, feeling *freeeeeeeeeeee*

Head and Arms

Painting: Standing in a wide circle, dip your arms into imaginary jars of paint. Then using them as brushes make designs in the air—high, low, circular—curving to make the designs open and free. Your body shows the flow of paint. Sometimes paint sweeps across the canvas in wide swaths; sometimes it drips down;

Figure 10.3 Feeling big: Stretch high as you can, stand on your toes, raise your arms, and lift your eyes to the sky. Big . . . so big . . . beyond your body.

Credit line: Courtesy of Alice Teirstein.

sometimes it makes big dots and splashes. Your whole body is the paintbrush, and you've created color in all the space around you.

Baseball: Swing a bat, pitch balls, and catch a ball in slow motion. Slow way down and exaggerate every movement. Jump to catch a fly ball. Spin for a dazzling preparation at bat.

Figure 10.4 Baseball. Slow way down and exaggerate the movement of your body and the force of the ball.

Credit line: Courtesy of Judith Peck, camper at Camp Chateaugay, Merrill NY.

Showing sadness: Your head is downcast, your shoulders are rounded, your arms curve inward and away, and your body turns this way and that, not knowing where you want to go.

Showing happiness: Open your arms wide and high. Let your head lift and face side to side, your eyes seeing everything around you. Your arms reach out, hands touching everything. Why not contrast sad and happy movements, first one and then the other? That's the way things happen anyway.

Jewelry: Surprise! You've come upon a treasure chest on the beach, left there by pirates when they fled from police back to their boats. Open it and pull out handfuls of imaginary jewelry. There are bracelets—pull them down along your arms, scarves to wrap around your head and shoulders, hats of every shape: tall, pointed magician's hats, sparkling crowns for kings. People come to see what's going on, and you share the precious jewels with them, tossing the glittering gems to everyone.

Boxing: Box in partners or a group. Exaggerate the thrusts of your arms and fists. Magnify the "blows" that hit you with slow-motion pantomime. Practice several times, swinging a punch and receiving one. No actual touching or hitting allowed! Then one at a time with a partner, swing a big *imaginary* punch at him. He caves in or totters trying not to fall. Then he swings at you, and you cave in or spin around or almost fall—whatever you like to show the thrust of his swing. Do this combination several times, punching and getting punched. How inventive can you be to show the moves?

Magic wands: Your arms hold imaginary wands. The wands lead you in different directions. One wand leads you all the way to a far corner of the world and just when you return, the other wand leads you all the way to another corner. The wands like to play. One wand seems to lead you high up to the stars, while the other makes you curve very low as it takes you for a visit under the ground. (This image is meant to help children use all the space around them, end to end and high and low, as well as for developing fluidity of arm movements).

Cowboys (in partners): How does a cowboy throw a lasso? Take a partner who will play the part of the horse. Ready? Pull your arm way, way back across your chest; then sweep it forward and out as far as it will go. Did you loop it around the horse? If so, see your horse strain against the pull of the rope. Okay, then pull the lasso back to drag the horse where you want the straining animal to go. (The partners should create maximum tension between each other so there will appear to be a real rope connecting them.)

Rodeo: Wild broncos in a rodeo try to throw the cowboys riding them. You are one of those brave guys, competing to see how many minutes you can hold on to those reins and remain on the kicking, buckling bronco before falling off.

Western falls: "Ya got me!" Show dramatic ways you can fall. (Children should use maximum contrast of high to low movements and creative ways of hitting the dust.)

In the dark: Pretend to be groping in the dark using your arms to find the walls and doorway. Exaggerate your movements. Bump into furniture. Accidentally touch an icky spider web. Stub your toe. (An extension of this project is to interpret the textures one might feel in a dark room: sharp and pointy, rough and abrasive, silky smooth, etc.)

Torso

Window stretches: Stretch high with both arms, head high as if you are opening a window to let in the sunlight. Stretch low as if you are struggling to close a long low window. Repeat and alternate the gestures to create a dance of surprises. Let a big breeze come in to spin you around.

Rubber bands: S-t-r-e-t-c-h to one side and then to the other, in each case as if you were pulling a rubber band

Figure 10.5 Stretch as if opening a window, then pushing open a door, perhaps to catch the breeze and balmy smell of springtime.

Credit Line: Courtesy of CityStep.

as far as it will go. Repeat the same sequence of movements, but this time pretend the rubber band snaps, making you bounce back after each stretch.

Swings in place: The swing goes UP . . . Run forward, your arms swinging up and high, your head stretching to the sky. The swing goes DOWN . . . Run backward, your arms swinging backward and down, your body bent low. Increase the UP suspension with each repeat: Swing high and *h-o-l-d.* . . . Add a lift onto your toes at the last minute to increase suspension. *Then drop.* Repeat the sequences, changing the swing's direction. This imaginary swing can go anyplace you decide.

In and out: Improvise ideas that suggest something moving inwardly and something moving outwardly. For example, feeling sad and perhaps even crying would prompt inward movements, your body torso rounded, head down. Santa Claus, jolly and fat, laughing and tossing candy would prompt outward movements, open and broad. Being afraid, shy, or sick would arouse inward movements while feeling happy, bold, and free would inspire outward movements. Let your arms lead the rest of your body and take each movement to its fullest before contrasting it with a pull the opposite way.

Spreading roots: Kneeling or crouching or standing as you prefer, make fluid designs with your arms and body showing roots spreading out in several directions. One movement flows into another. You can support yourself on the floor with your hand and use a leg to extend out as well. Face different corners of the room without breaking the flow of movement. (Slow, sustained music or drum beats can help keep the tension and the flow of one reach moving into another.)

In the sun and in the shade: This sequence is best done on your knees on the floor for maximum invention and minimum need for balance. Use high, open movements for the sun, arching your back and lifting your chest; for the shade, use low, rounded movements. Alternate the two images letting one flow into the other with reaching and receding motions. (A drum is useful to build loud, dominant beats for the sun and soft, slow rhythms for the shade.)

"Ooof!": Kneel high on your knees with arms raised. Someone throws an imaginary ball causing you to cave in at the waist—"Ooof!" Slowly recover to come up high as before. Again a big ball is thrown, and again, there is a cave in followed by a recovery. Make variations of this contraction and release, bending to the side as well as forward and backward. Put a hand on the floor for support and try extending a leg in the air on one of the releases. Everything is down and inward on the contraction; everything is high and open on the release.

Spaghetti cooked and uncooked: Contrast curvy, circular movements with straight movements of your torso and arms. Try creating this contrast in partners, one child weaving in rounded circular patterns around the other who is standing or jumping with the sharp, straight, crisp feel of spaghetti before it hits the pot. The whole group can "cook" together beginning rigid then loosening . . . until everyone splashes into the colander!

Clay: Slowly stretch yourself into an interesting form as if emerging from a mound of clay. Then merge into a different form. (As a variation, one child can be the sculptor directing the actions and the other the forms created.)

Shapes: Point out ordinary items you see around you or think of them from memory and talk about its shape. Is it round, square, rectangular, pointed, twisted, straight-edged, smooth? Look out the window at buildings, roads, pathways, trees, and natural phenomena. Observe their forms and shapes. Then interpret these shapes in movement. This project is fun to do in partners or in groups. It can also be a guessing game: you or your group secretly select an object and interpret it while the others guess what it is by its shape. Clues as to its use will help and can be given in movement pantomime (or verbally) as you wish.

Twisting vines: Show how the vines twist in and out, high and low along arbors, trees, and buildings. Show the tension, pulling and stretching as the "vines" twist and climb, gripping anything they can get hold of. (If this is done in groups the children can weave around each other; if done in partners, one might be the vine, the other the tree getting tangled in the vine. Do the twisting motions without actually touching.)

Reference List for Class Sessions
Movements in Place—Middle of the Room

Legs and Feet

Trees and branches in heavy wind
Brooms sweeping
Obedient muscles
Jumps, hops, balancing
Shoes, boots, slippers, skates, and paws

Head and Arms

Painting
Feeling big
Baseball—pitcher, batter, catcher (partners)
Boxing (in partners)
Rodeo
Cowboys lassoing horses (partners)
Hats
Magic wands
Stumbling in the dark
Sadness
Happiness
Sparkling jewelry

Torso—Standing

Morning stretches
Rubber bands
Swings in place
Weaving in and out
Shape-making
Spaghetti, cooked and uncooked (partners)
Twisted vines (partners)

Torso—Kneeling

Spreading roots
In the sun/in the shade

"Ooof!" Belly punches
Clay creations

Broad Movements Around and Across the Room

Circular Moves

Ripples in the water
Paint cans
Musical tunes
Turns and Twists
Spots before your eyes
Lost in the woods
Finding a surprise
Exploring pictures in a museum

Movements High, Low, and In-Between

Stars
Fireflies
Snakes
Sneaky witch
Visiting imaginary lands
Rope pull (opposing groups)

Movements Straight-Ahead

Pony trots
Circus ponies
Racehorse
Birds soaring in the air
Skips
Leaping—over tall grass in a field
Running forward—gusts of wind
Running backward—away from an oncoming bear
Running sideways—lost in the forest
All over ethe place—scribbling
Racing—late for school
Running and stopping—bees flying among flowers

Directional Changes—side to side, forward to back

A lost canary
Leaves in the wind

 Surprises
 Runaway swings
 Butterfly landing
 Playing hide and seek

The time spent on any of these activities will be determined by the attention span of the children involved and the demands of existing schedules. All the suggested images can be used as suggested or expanded to suit the interests of the group or changed completely, using them simply as points of departure.

11 Flight Patterns

The Launching

Interesting and well-balanced movements in space can be compared with the designs an artist makes on paper or canvas. A busy dance done in one place on a large floor lacks design and balance just as a painting does when executed on only a small portion of a large canvas. It is a good idea to illustrate this to the children by actually drawing a design on a large sheet of paper using only one corner and leaving the rest of the paper empty. Then make a similar design using all the paper and contrast the two. The children will be quick to tell you which picture is better.

Movement in space refers essentially to three things in the context of these projects:

How in the Space to Move

Inward
Outward
Forward
Backward
Upward
Downward
Sideward
Circularly

Where in the Space to Move

Along the width
Along the depth

DOI: 10.4324/9781003254812-14

Along the diagonals
Around the center

Levels in Which to Move

High (stretching, jumping, leaping, skipping)
Low (crouching, bending, kneeling, creeping, slinking,
    sneaking)
In between (walking, running, sliding, reaching arms,
    extending a leg, turning)

Balance, design, and contrast will evolve if these principles
of moving in space are kept in mind. It is not necessary to
plan spatial patterns in advance unless demanded by a specific project. Good spatial patterns will appear spontaneously
once the children know what to try for.

Space is the medium for creative movement, just as paint
and clay are mediums for visual art. Children should understand the full range and possibilities so they can use it advantageously as their medium of expression.

In the pages that follow, ideas are given that relate to spatial movement. Additional projects on spatial design are
found in Chapter 15 Improvisations on the arts.

How and Where to Go

Gusts of wind: Pretend to be propelled forward by a
    strong gust of wind. With arms held out to the sides,
    chest lifted, and head held high, wait for the imaginary
    feeling of the wind behind you. Then run across the
    floor, chest leading. (A gentle push in the small of the
    back can help children get started.)
Don't slow down!: Run backward across the floor as if flee-
    ing from something (ask the children to suggest what),
    not slowing down. Swift peeks over the shoulder are fine.
    (For preschool children, the leader can wait at the oppo-
    site end and catch them as they come across.)
Lost in the forest: Pretend to be lost in a forest of tall
    trees, searching for a way out. Cross from one corner to

another, peering out across the trees to find the path-way home. Make the most of each long gaze into the distance by stretching your arms out as if it is difficult to see past the trees.

Ripples in the water: The leader pretends to throw stones into an imaginary lake. The children, as if they were the ripples in the water, move circularly in wider and wider patterns. The arms lead the body as it bends into the curve of the circles.

Spots before your eyes: In a line formation, face a colorful object or spot on the wall opposite, some point of focus everyone can clearly see. Using your arms for balance and thrust, turn in place, keeping eyes fixed on it. For one brief moment as you turn, your eyes must leave the spot, but they return to it at once. This focus and snapping motion of the head will prevent dizziness as you turn.

Scribbling: Each child, pretending to be a pencil, is put through an imaginary pencil sharpener (by the leader

Figure 11.1 Pretend to be lost in a forest of tall trees searching for a way out.

Credit line: Photo by Erik Unhjem.

Figure 11.2 Paint cans. Jump into an imaginary can of paint and emerge to make designs in space.

Credit line: Courtesy of Alice Teirstein.

or another child). The sharpened pencils are turned loose on the paper (in the room) to scribble designs. Use all the available space—high, low, and in between—from corner to corner and end to end of the room.

Paint cans: Jump into an imaginary can of paint, and splash paint all over your body. Dunk your head as well.

Emerge to make magnificent designs. Use your whole body and all the available space. Change directions as your bold arms, feet, and head movements create the brush strokes. The paint can be any color and the stokes can be stripes, polka dots, swirls, or whatever you like. In the imagination, anything is possible!

Pictures: Everyone is given paper and pencil and is asked to draw an interesting balanced design using vertical, horizontal, diagonal, and circular lines. Following this, the design on the paper is transferred to movement in space. This is best done individually. Each child props up his or her drawing where it is easily seen while moving. The design is then performed by walking, running, or dancing.

Any manner of embellishments can be made on this project by adding crayons, colored pencils, or magic markers. The project can also be reversed. The children can be asked to make a drawing or colored picture based on a dance improvisation.

Running "oofs": Pretend that you are catching a large beach ball that forces you to cave in and to run backward. First toss the ball away and follow it in a forward direction. Catch the ball, then "oof!" Cave in and run backwards. Repeat catching the ball and caving in but vary your backward direction to include diagonals and zigzags. Do the same with your forward direction.

Levels of Movement

High

The lost canary: An imaginary canary is lost somewhere in the room. It is obviously high up. Look for the canary with high movements that take you in many directions all about the room.

Stars: It is night. You are up late and outside on a summer night. You stare up at the starlit sky and imagine what's up there. Your body gets the question and begins to dance, moving brightly to show the luminous stars. Fast, high, sparkling movements show the twinkling stars. Then, because it is late, you yawn, stretch high and wide, and then lie down, right there, as if to sleep.

Fireflies: This story is similar to "Stars," but this time the children are out at night to see the fireflies. Your movements improvise to show the on–off flickering of the firefly lights—out and in, up and down. Fireflies race all around one another: on–off, up–down, in–out.

Low

Beetle bug: An imaginary beetle bug is lost somewhere on the floor. Investigate all corners; travel close to the ground (though not lying on it); use your arms to make wide searching movements.

Snakes: Curl up in a ball then straighten and extend your back, neck, and head with a *hiss.* Curl and uncurl in different ways, undulating like a snake.

Witch: A mean witch plotting evil deeds moves low around a bubbling cauldron. She makes weird voodoo sounds as she stirs the pot.

Using All Levels—High, Low, and In Between

Visiting imaginary lands: This is a game that children love to play, and since it uses all the levels and contrasts, it is an excellent project for the first session (see the many lands below). Sitting in a circle on the floor, the children first choose and then discuss an imaginary land that they would like to visit. Following this, they stand together and interpret the things they would likely see there.

Interpret each imaginary land together dancing any of the things you would likely see there. After the "trip," return to the circle and discuss the next imaginary land to be visited and what you would be seeing. Then stand and together interpret those in movement, all the different beings and objects together.

The following is a brief list of imaginary lands that children have "visited" in the past, including the animals, bugs, nature, and objects encountered:

- Low land: moles, tree roots, carrots, snakes, worms, flower roots, rabbit holes, sewers, tunnels
- High land: clouds, stars, trees, birds, moon, God, wind, sun, butterflies, skyscrapers, airplanes, rockets
- Whisper land: mice, kittens, children when a parent is on the telephone, wind, secrets
- Screaming land: lions, tigers, arguing people, fog horns, sirens, jets taking off, traffic noises.
- Hoppity land: rabbits, kangaroos, grasshoppers, happy children
- Jumpity land: jack-in-the-box, busy people, jacks, jumping beans, frightened people, puppets, nervous people
- Silly land: clowns, some children, monkeys
- Sad land: sick people, hurt animals, punished children, wilted flowers
- Jolly land: balls and toys, cartoons, clowns, carnivals, Santa Claus
- Wet land: people caught in the rain, flowers and branches drooping from heavy rain, snow slush, bird baths, lawn sprinklers.

Leaves in the wind: You can move as either wind or leaves. The wind blows at the leaves (use your body moving not your mouth blowing). The leaves are scattered low along the ground and high in the air. Sometimes the leaves lie quietly, and sometimes they travel with sudden changes of direction as the wind blows them about. The wind pushes forward and lashes out to the side. Sometimes it swirls around like you imagine a tornado might do. The project is fun to do in partners.

Late for school: Look for your hat high on a shelf somewhere, or is it in another room down the hall? Look for your boots—hidden under something in a closet maybe? Grab your jacket off a hook and put it on. Drat! It's your brother's. Take it off and sling it back on the hook.

Figure 11.3 Exploring contrasts. A boy reaches forward and crouches low as if to catch a swirl of falling leaves while behind him a girl reaches high as if to greet the stars.

Credit Line: Courtesy of CityStep.

Remember, you're in a hurry! Keep alternating the levels high, low, and in between and travel all over. Tardy again, darn it!

Surprises: A game that makes use of all the levels. Each series is done across the floor, alternating the walk and the surprise in a rhythmic fashion. Show the surprise by stopping sharply in a pose or by a sudden movement on whatever level is indicated.

- A surprise from overhead: Pretend to be walking down the street when suddenly you hear an explosion above you, or you see a shooting star or a fantastic bird. Exaggerate your movement.
- A surprise from straight-ahead: Your casual walk is interrupted by a sudden shout from the distance or by a strange sight directly in front of you. It stops you short, almost falling backward.
- A surprise from behind: Whirl around as if someone suddenly called out to you or a blast sounded behind you. This surprise can inspire interesting turns on a high or low plane.

Rope pull: Two lines of children face each other about a yard apart. Children in one line have imaginary ropes around them that their opponents in the opposite line are pulling. Slowly, with great tension hold the ropes and pull your straining opponents toward you. Pull on high, low, and in-between levels as you work to upset the other side. Stretch your legs and change your stance frequently for more strength. Pull and balance your body so you don't give in and drop the rope. Your opponents resist being pulled, pushing hard against the imaginary rope. No one wins; the rope does not break; no one falls in a heap on top of everyone else. Or do they? Up to you.

Runaway swings: Bend forward head down, arms behind you; run across the floor, swinging your arms forward and up and lifting your head high. Stay high on your toes without moving, as if suspended. Then drop your head and arms down and run backward. Repeat this,

Figure 11.4 A surprise from behind. Whirl around as if someone suddenly calls out to you or a blast sounds from
behind.

Credit line: Courtesy of Alice Teirstein.

moving in many different directions of the room but
always going forward from low to high, staying for a
moment and then dropping your arms and going backward. Add high turns sometimes after swinging forward

and low turns after swinging backward. You can then interpret the following story:

The swings in the playground became weary of going forward and backward, forward and backward, always in the same place, always in the same way. They decided to run away, to swing anywhere they wanted to, in any way they wanted to. And so they did!

Part IV

Improvisations

Figure 12.0 Once a child interprets the seed growing and pushing through the earth forming a stem, leaf, and at last a flower, he has a kinship with that mystery.

Credit line: Courtesy of Alice Teirstein.

DOI: 10.4324/9781003254812-15

12 Getting Started

Group Discussions

Seated together in an informal arrangement, either on the floor or on chairs in a circle, the project to be interpreted is thoroughly discussed. This discussion is the principal means of awakening perceptions and provoking thought. The process of children articulating their thoughts is essential not only to the success of each project but also to the productive participation of each child. The children focus on the subject, crystallize their thoughts, and contribute ideas that are discussed in the group. This group recognition of the validity of their ideas increases the desire of children to probe the subject further with the added self-confidence to do so. The relationship between self-confidence and the assumption of validity in one's perceptions is not restricted to children. A great deal of the natural perceptive abilities in us all is overlooked because of a lack of confidence in our observations. Every writer you have ever read could not have put words to paper without that assumption of validity. The group discussions may sharpen your own perceptions if you consciously make the effort to focus on the issue and verbally share your impressions.

It is reassuring to know as you stare into a sea of expectant faces that the ideas are there in abundance just waiting to be pulled ashore. Remember you are offering an experience that the children's brains will retain with understanding beyond what their eyes have seen. For example, once a child interprets the seed growing and pushing through the

DOI: 10.4324/9781003254812-16

earth, forming a stem, leaves, and at last a flower, they have a kinship with that mystery they might not otherwise have had.

Some of the following methods may be helpful in stimulating the initial discussions:

- Asking leading questions
- Stating your personal experiences and asking the children for theirs
- Using pictorial and literary material found in magazines, poems, photographs, and online descriptions

Suggesting your own ideas may make it easier to launch a project initially. In all likelihood, these ideas may not be needed after a few sessions.

Group Improvisations

While the discussion continues, the subject matter is explored through movement. For example, if the project is "A Walk in New York City," you might ask how one could show a skyscraper. A child volunteering might rise slowly from a low position and tower with arms angular to show the geometric outlines of the building. As other sights are suggested and discussed, they are also interpreted. In this project there might be police directing traffic, automobiles and buses, trucks and delivery bikes, men of the sanitation department dumping huge vats of rubbish into their trucks. The demonstrations are made by one child at a time or several or all the children together.

The leader should participate verbally by throwing out some of these ideas to expand the improvisations while the children are moving. She can also demonstrate movements as she speaks. Often, a child will do a fragment of a movement that has a good possibility for development. These opportunities should be watched for. Let's say, for example, a child showing a traffic police officer raises his hand, then turns to face a different side. This movement can be exaggerated. The first part can become a jump and the second a spin. The whole group is asked to participate in expanding movements such as these.

An actual police officer's traffic direction as it might appear on the street is not to be imitated, it is to be creatively interpreted. The distinction between imitation and creative interpretation should be emphasized. Children must understand the difference between trying to look like something and trying to interpret it. If a boy slithers along the floor to portray a snake, he can never convince us that he is really a snake, nor does he want to. At best he might only present a simple imitation in this fashion. To make an original improvisation of a snake, the child must use his body and the space around him in the most dynamic human way possible and wriggling on the floor limits his capacity to do this. The objective is not to imitate the reptile, insect or animal but to create movements inspired by it, worthwhile on their own terms.

After the experimental improvisations, there are two ways of proceeding, in one group or in several groups. The number of participants involved will surely affect which method of improvisation to use as will the age of the participants. In some situations, it may be possible to have older children on hand to sit in with a group of young children to help guide the improv.

One Group

The entire group can do the project together. First, parts are chosen by the children. To use the illustration "A Walk in New York City," all those who want to do the skyscrapers raise their hands, then all those who want to do police officers, buses, motorcycles, and so on raise their hands and are chosen. Usually children are agreeable to changing their choice of parts when there are too many for one and not enough for another. The characters then take their places on the floor or go to separate corners of the room and await their appropriate moment of entry. The project is announced either by the leader or by one of the children to an imaginary audience.

Then the story or project is narrated by the leader (ad lib) and the children do their parts spontaneously as they occur.

Several Groups

An alternate procedure is to have the children form small groups. This procedure is recommended when you are dealing with a large number of children at one time. In small groups, they will have more opportunities to contribute ideas. Also, some children are not motivated to contribute ideas to the class as a whole, but when they are among friends, they feel a sense of teamwork and put forth effort that would otherwise not appear. Another advantage is that the children have a chance to see other ways of interpreting the same subject. In situations in which there is a large age difference among the children, the procedure of several groups serves the purpose of allowing older children to work separately from younger ones or to disperse among them to help.

To proceed, the leader asks the children to form groups consisting of approximately three to nine people or she forms them herself. The groups meet in separate corners of the room to plan their respective ways of presenting the project, the leader going from group to group throughout the planning period to help. Each improvisation will probably take about 5 minutes.

Planning the Improvisation

1. Choose a *title*.
2. Choose *parts* and select an announcer who in addition to having a part in the group presentation will announce the title and characters.
3. Make a general *plan*. It will probably be little more than an idea. For example, in the project "A Walk in New York City," the group might decide to show a woman in high heels walking a dog and children playing ball. At the same time, they might show an interpretation of tall

buildings in the background and perhaps a subway. If the group is more mature or adventurous, they might make up a story within the theme: Perhaps the ball accidentally hits the lady, causing the dog to chase the children, and then a police officer appears to take them all to the station house for disturbing the peace.

4. *Add sound effects (if you wish).* Some children may be hesitant to do any improvisations. This is an opportunity to engage them in the production by making sound effects. These can be via their own voices whirring or groaning or hooting—whatever—or via drumbeats on hands or floor or actual drums or music streamed on a smartphone or other recording device. However produced, sound effects can be helpful to ease self-consciousness and inspire movement. If no one in the participant group is involved, the leader can create the effects with ideas from the children as to what sounds to produce at what time in the improvisation.

5. Take a *beginning pose* so the project will have some structure. This pose should have balance and design. For example, the buildings in the background should appear tall and the subway stretching out low and vibrating. The ball players freeze in an action pose related to throwing or catching. The lady and her dog are in a corner "offstage," ready to trot in. The characters "onstage" should not bunch together but should try to make an interesting composition of their beginning pose.

6. Design an *ending pose.* This may be a repeat of the beginning pose.

7. All the previously mentioned things are done by the group members themselves with help provided by the leader. A note of encouragement: Have confidence! The children will come up with something you can be sure and with the applause from the other groups at the end (which the leader initiates), be quite proud of themselves. Nevertheless, this is the moment you might consider your gloomiest. What if nothing comes? What if it falls flat? But you see, things are looking up already. In Part III, you

thought this about yourself. What if nothing comes? What if I fall flat? But you didn't, and neither will this.

8. When the time allowed for planning is up—probably 10 or 15 minutes—each group faces the "performing" area to watch. Unless the groups express specific desires to go first, last, or in the middle, the leader decides on the order in which the groups perform. Then each group in turn takes its starting pose, presents its improvisations, and concludes with an interesting final pose. A bow tips off the applause that the leader initiates and the watching groups should pick up with gusto.

Summary of Things for Children to Remember

1. Express the subject matter as well as possible.
2. Balance the stage. Obviously balance is weak if everyone is clustered on one side of the floor.
3. Contrast movements if you can—your own as well as in the group composition, for example, high, low, open, closed, fast, slow, and so on.
4. Use all parts of your body in moving, your head as well.
5. Vary directions in space: length (across the floor), depth (from front to back of the floor), and diagonal (from corner to corner).
6. Vary directions of your body: forward, backward, sideward, inward, outward, and circular.
7. Relate to one another out of the corner of your eye. Think about the improv as a performance in which each person moving is a part of an artistic composition.

Ways to Present the Improvisation

The leader or the individual groups can choose to have the titles of the improvisations guessed by the "audience." This adds an element of fun and holds the attention of those watching and waiting their turn to perform. To do this, members of the audience raise their hands after the interpretation is completed and are called on to guess what each person or the group as a whole represented.

Alternatively, the actual interpretation of the idea or situation can be given in advance. This would be done where the improvisation needs more definition, such as, for example, in the project "Colors," to stimulate more creative participation from those watching.

13 Improvisations on Nature

A treasure of material to unearth for movement interpretation is here for the plowing. Nature itself is on the move, all the time, and your body is the perfect shape and kinesthetic instrument to experience its improvisations. Give some thought to your observations in the daily routines you do outdoors. Look up high, down low, and all about, and you will doubtless discover other aspects in nature to explore beyond the ones described here. Remember that each project begins with everyone sitting down, talking, and contributing ideas about the scene being visualized. When the improvisations are presented, they can be *announced* in advance to the watching groups or *guessed* as to what is being interpreted (A or G).

> **Changes and transitions:** Think about elements in nature that change their form, for example, water into ice and then ice into puddles of water and what elements cause these changes. Describe together all the transitions you can think of. Experiment with ways of translating these changes into creative movement, then divide into groups and present some of these transitions (*A* or G).
>
> **Metamorphosis:** Discuss the metamorphosis of a caterpillar to the cocoon and then to the emerging butterfly. Stand, and although you may be moving with others, create individual ways to show these transformations. Alternatively, take turns or work in groups, choosing separate transformations.

DOI: 10.4324/9781003254812-17

Discuss other remarkable metamorphosis in nature like the tadpole to the frog and create your movement interpretation of this. Pictures of these amphibians would be good to have on hand.

> **Planting seeds:** Everyone scatters and lands on the floor as the leader *pretends* to throw them from different packets of seed. By prearrangement or by whispering in their ears while they are on the floor, the children begin to grow, develop, and blossom according to the kind of seed they represent.
>
> **Trees:** Beginning very low, everyone moves like tree roots spreading under the ground. If it is to be a big tree such as an oak, the roots must go very far in a few directions to support it. The tree begins to grow, very slowly, and branches form twisted and irregular shapes. The tree trunk becomes strong. Leaves grow from the branches in the spring. When autumn comes the leaves turn fiery colors. Toward winter, the leaves dry up and crackle as the wind sends them crumbling to the ground. Think about how your arms, hands, legs, head, and body can interpret these elements.

There are many stories about trees that lend themselves to creative interpretation. "The Littlest Evergreen" is one. Using the tree to show changes in nature presents wonderful opportunities because all four seasons—atmospheric elements, insects, birds, and animals—share in its story.

A nature walk: If the situation allows, the leader and the children go for a walk out of doors. Point out to one another aspects of nature that interest you and talk about their texture, shape, and color and how they move. The leader might make a list of the things observed in both flower and fauna. Think about how you can experience what you are seeing by moving your body in space. Creative movement in the open air is fun: leaps on an open field, stretches and turns among the trees. But if the situation is not conducive to being outside, the ideas can be collected and brought inside.

Figure 13.1 The tree image is excellent for showing changes in nature because all four seasons—atmospheric elements, insects, birds, and animals—share in its story.

Credit line: Photo by Erik Unhjem.

Figure 13.2 The tree grows very slowly, forming branches in twisted and irregular shapes.

Credit line: Courtesy of Alice Teirstein.

Individually or in groups, choose something seen on the walk to interpret creatively. Observations will include worms, insects, shoots, flowers, birds, twigs, and so on. The improvisations can be guessed at by others. If it is not possible to go on a nature walk, as in most instances it probably will not, an imaginary walk can be taken. Walk around the room, pretending to see one thing or another, then divide into groups as above and interpret your observations. You might improvise a story around the object. For example, interpreting bees, a group can dramatize this: A bee takes nectar from a flower, turns away to chase a boy, and finally stings him. If one has a flair for melodrama, the bee's demise can be included.

Twigs: This is another project for actually doing out of doors. Look for twigs with interesting shapes and collect them. Back inside, place the twig where you can see it clearly, and moving in place try to form your body into its curves. Some twigs might give you ideas beyond their shape. For example, one twig might have the shape of fire, another a monster, another an animal, and so on. Interpretations can be done individually or in groups, to be announced in advance or guessed as to what is represented (*A* or G).

In the ground, in the sky, in the water: Discuss together things that move in each of these areas and then interpret the ideas on a low or high plane according to the category. For example:

- In the ground: roots, moles, rabbits, worms, subways, tunnels, pipes
- In the sky: clouds, stars, moon, sun, birds, planes, rockets, space labs
- In the water: seaweed, fish, swimmers, boats, submarines, snails, shells.

Groups can select separate categories and interpret several examples in each one.

Note: "The Visits" is a story that can accompany this project.

Mountain climbing: This project is best done in one group. The children begin low to the floor, then slowly rise, interpreting some of the things they would see while climbing a mountain. Examples of mountain activity are goats, wildflowers, rocks, snakes, berries, trees, deer, snow, skiers, vines, mountain streams, and jagged cliffs. To stimulate movement, the leader can claim to see some of these things as the children move.

Growth and overgrowth: Contrast the growth of the same vegetation according to its environment and its nurture. For example, blades of grass can grow in an orderly fashion on your lawn to be neatly clipped down each week by the mower, or grass can grow tall and thick in a field, or wild and entangled in the swamp.

Clouds: Discuss and adapt any of the following to fit the interests and level of the children assembled.

- Search the clouds, observing their shapes, shadows, and patterns for movement ideas.
- Study the different types of clouds—cirrus, cumulus, nimbus, and stratus—and try to form distinctive ways to distinguish each through movements and movement patterns in space.
- The children in one group secretly select the kind of day they want it to be. They then interpret how the clouds would behave on that day. The children in another group pretend to look at the clouds overhead (decide what they see) and pattern their day accordingly. For example, slow drifting clouds might enable them to skip to the fields and play ball; dark threatening clouds might make them run for cover. Gentle skies might send them to the lake for a row then have them battling the waves if the clouds suddenly burst open. And clouds can do that!

Things that go up and down: Discuss and then improvise movements to convey the following ideas:

- things that *rise slowly* (gas-filled balloons, smoke, birds, the sun, a kite, a spider crawling on its web)

Figure 13.3 Weeds and grass untended can grow wild and high and cascade down in curves and tangles. Create a group movement picture of this.

Credit line: Photo by Erik Unhjem.

Figure 13.4 Search the clouds for movement ideas, observing their shapes, lights and shadows, and patterns.

Credit line: Photo by Erik Unhjem.

- things that *rise quickly* (a ball, rock, jet, rocket, jack-in-the-box, water jetting from a fountain)
- things that *descend slowly* (a wilting flower, dew, mist, a feather, a bird landing, the sun)
- things that *descend quickly* (apples falling from a tree, a person tripping, rain, a waterfall, a ball falling into a mitt)
- Divide into groups for improvisations in the category of your choice. After this, choose two categories simultaneously to create interesting contrasts in height and tempo (*A* or *G*).

Bugs and such: First discuss and then in pairs show movement relationships of insects to people and to other insects. Use the following scenarios as a start:

1. Devise ways to show characteristic movements of bugs on a low level for crawling insects and on a high level for

Figure 13.5 There's so much to wonder about in nature—way too high to touch and too underground to see, but all your own to imagine.

Credit line: Courtesy of CityStep.

flying ones. Some interesting "bugs and such" for this are ants, spiders, caterpillars, worms, flies, and bees. Show attacks on one another using the movement contrasts of bugs that are high and those that are low.

2. Show the relationships of insects to other insects moving on the same plane, such as the spider catching the fly in its web. This will be fun for sure.

3. Discuss and show conflicting relationships of insects to people and to nature: for example, insects as pests and insects as workers. Schoolwork on this subject can be used advantageously.

Construction: Show the construction of man-made projects that affect nature such as dams, tunnels, bridges, and roads. Exaggerate movements to show the methods and equipment used to erect buildings, the hazards of weather and falling debris for workers, the changes to a skyline caused by the construction, and possibly the ultimate function of each construction project. Short "action" stories can be devised and dramatized.

14 Improvisations on the Seasons

We are as familiar with the dependable changes we acclimate ourselves to in the four seasons as we are to the variations of character in our family members, schoolmates, colleagues, and even our pets. But experiencing the seasons through thoughtful improvisations can provide new insights relevant to our lives. At present, with global warming and climate change affecting every corner of our vulnerable universe, it is timely to be sensitive to the ceaseless natural changes that exist in the world we live in and cognizant of the unnatural ones already in our midst.

Spring

Signs of spring: In the discussion period, children are asked to think of familiar signs of spring and call them out. There would be the appearance of certain kinds of birds, the growth of flowers and plants, the beginning of baseball season, the balmy spring breeze.

Then everyone goes to the window. The leader and children together observe and talk about the signs of spring they see. The leader expands on their characteristics verbally in preparation for the movement interpretations that come next.

As indicated in the previous section, the leader and children then move to show specific signs of spring one at a time. After this, the children divide into groups. Each group decides on its own sign of spring to present to the class. For example, one group might do an interpretation of

DOI: 10.4324/9781003254812-18

bees taking pollen from the flowers while another is planting a garden and watching the seeds germinate. Following a brief planning session, they present to the other groups their improvisation. The form for this can be a simple story about what's going on, which is announced in advance, or presented as a guessing game. (A or G).

Pictures of spring: Crayons and paper are necessary. Each child draws a picture relating to spring. Then individually or in groups the pictures are made to "come to life."

Catching butterflies: One or more children represent butterflies, while others follow with imaginary nets lifting, flipping, and swooping down trying to catch them. Remember that the object is not really to catch the butterfly but to use this image as an aid in creating interesting movements. It works better if the children do not actually touch each other.

Flying kites: In partners, some children represent kites and some the wind. The kites move smoothly when the wind is calm but buffet about when the wind becomes rough. A variation of this project is to have some children be the kite fliers, pulling on imaginary strings. This is best done in partners. When one child pulls in their strings, the corresponding kite must move toward them. When the strings are let out, the kite drifts away. Maximum tension between the partners should be created to make the relationship effective. (A).

March winds: In groups or partners, some children portray the March wind and others some of the things on which wind blows. The children will suggest combinations such as wind and trees, wind and flowers, wind and people, wind and water, wind and boats, wind and umbrellas. (A or G).

Baseball: Improvisations on batting, pitching, catching, running bases, and sliding. Exaggerate all movements. Slow motion helps. (A or G).

Summer

Water: The many different forms of water are discussed and then interpreted. The following is a list of suggestions (A or G):

waterfall	bathing water	ice
whirlpool	ocean	lakes
swimming pool	brooks	bird baths
drinking water	rivers	streams
snow	rain	fountain
dew	steam	geysers

Remember that the characteristics of each form of water must be exaggerated. (Take a great deal of artistic liberty.)

Discuss together some of the different forms water can take and then interpret these forms together exaggerating their characteristics.

Consider working in partners. For example, in a waterfall, make a dance of the plunging water and the rising spray.

Carnivals and Fairs: Discuss the kinds of booths, rides, food, people, pets, vehicles you might see in a summer carnival (A or G).

Summer activities: Discuss and then interpret the activities that occupy children during the summer when they are out of school. Each improvisation should be pantomimed in broad slow motion showing inventively the essential movements:

In the city: ball playing, fire hydrant blasts of water; playground activities on the slides, jungle gym, swings, and seesaws; jump ropes, roller skating, running with the dog

In the country: bike riding, horseback riding, tennis, ball playing, rowing, swimming, setting up tents and gathering wood for camping, gardening, hiking, fishing

Use slow-motion and exaggerate your movements to give your body time to invent the shapes. (When a child has a particularly expressive movement for an activity, the leader might pick it up for the class to execute.) (A or G).

Sun: In partners or in groups, interpret some of the effects of the hot summer sun: its effect on people, making them thirsty, sending them splashing in a swimming pool or dashing through an open hydrant.

Figure 14.1 Lake water curves around an irregular shoreline, splashes against the rocks and with change in the wind becomes turbulent.

Credit line: Photo by Erik Unhjem.

Moving across the floor, show the contrast of feeling cold (rounded, inward, shivering movements) and feeling hot (open, languid stretches, and turns).

Flowers blooming: Curl up close to the floor as if under the ground. With low movements, extend arms and legs in changing directions to show the roots spreading out (as in

Figure 14.2 A waterfall plunges down the rocks and the falling
water creates thrashing foam and high-rising spray.

Credit line: Photo by Erik Unhjem.

the project "Vines"). With head and arms reaching high,
show the passage of the stem through the earth into the
open air, growing toward the sun. Balancing on one leg and
then on the other, make patterns in the air with the legs and
arms to show the leaves. The whole body creates the climax
of the open flower, arms high and eyes to the ceiling. Turns

can show the opening of the blossom. (Children should try to keep their shoulders down as they lift their arms high; it is effective to suggest that the blossom needs plenty of air around it to open fully, and one must not squash it.)

Telling the following story while the children move, may prove helpful. Allow enough time for each phase of the action:

> Slowly the roots spread out in many directions beneath the ground. A shoot begins to form and grow. It gently pushes the earth away to make room. The stem grows higher and higher, rising slowly, searching for the sun and rain to give it nourishment. Beautiful green leaves begin to form. At last the bud begins to open. Slowly the lovely petals appear, spreading wide to show their textures and their color.

Note: The theme of the story can be expanded during the telling by allowing some children to be flowers, some rain, and some the sunlight. (See "Baby Bud," in Part V, a story about flowers.)

Autumn

Colors of the autumn leaves: Interpret the vivid orange, yellow and red colors on trees, bushes, and shrubs by swirling your arms and reaching out as if making intricate patterns in space. Add leaps and turns. Show the colored leaves falling with slow-moving drops from high to low and fluttering moves across the floor. (A picture of autumn leaves is helpful to inspire movement.)

Fire: First discuss the attributes of fire; how it spreads, what it does—constructively and destructively—how it is used, how it is controlled, and so on. A way to start is with all the children crouched low. The music or drum indicates the lighting of the match, and the children rise slowly, twisting their bodies and shooting their arms in all directions as flames dart out and the smoke rises. (Again, pictures might be useful, but children are asked to close their eyes and imagine a blazing fire.) Some variations on fire are

- rain coming down to put the fire out,
- wind stimulating the fire to blaze,
- dancing in celebration around the fire,
- cold people warming themselves by the fire, and
- leaves crumpling and burning in the fire.

Note: See "The Speed and Fury of Fire," in Part V, a story about wind, rain, and fire (A or G).

Scampering leaves: A look out the window would probably reveal at least some leaves dropping from trees or already

Figure 14.3 Interpreting fire, the children jump high and twist their bodies and shoot their arms in many directions as flames dart and smoke rises.

Credit line: Courtesy of Alice Teirstein.

on the ground, perhaps sent into lively movement by a gust of wind. Some children can interpret the wind; some, the leaves, or all can be the leaves together. Show the leaves rustling in place, moving slowly close to the ground, or flying suddenly across the room.

Football: Do improvisations on tackling, kicking, catching, running with the ball, going into the huddle. Encourage

Figure 14.4 Interpreting football. Improvise movements of tackling, kicking, catching, and running with the ball. Exaggerate with pantomime, but no actual touching allowed.

Credit line: Photo by Erik Unhjem.

Figure 14.5 The feel of icicles is sharp, cold, jagged-edged, smooth-
surfaced, hard, slippery, and wet, and the look is sil-
very and sparkling.

Credit line: Photo by Erik Unhjem.

interesting movements by dividing boys into partners and
having one pretend to block while the other tries to throw.
Exaggerate movements in slow pantomime. No actual touching is allowed, or the whole group will end in a heap on
the floor. Cheerleading can be pantomimed as well. For this,
show lots of elevations of low to high and animated arm and
head movements (to energize the fans).

Winter

The feel and look of icicles: First, discuss as a group the feel of icicles, which is sharp, cold, jagged-edged but smooth-surfaced, hard, slippery, and wet. Then discuss the look—silver, shiny, and sparkling. Imagine both and make icicles happen in movement. You can choose to be sharp and jagged like the edges or smooth and slippery like the ice surface. Twist your body and bend your arms and legs to interpret the jagged shapes and create slow, lyrical movements to show the smooth, cold surface. You need not remain in place; jagged runs and sharp leaps across the floor can also convey the distinctive feel of icicles.

Snowflakes: The children know that each snowflake, amazing as it seems, is unique. This concept might inspire them to create original movements to represent snowflake shapes. Actual pictures of magnified snowflakes are helpful. The slow way snowflakes fall can make for interesting patterns of descent.

In a large group, create a variation: first just two or three snowflakes appear, fluttering in downward movements across the floor. Then others join, a few at a time, for this is how it happens. Then all the snowflakes are in the space, fluttering downward and all across the floor, thicker and thicker as no flakes can be seen, only snow. Children arrive scooting across in all manner of sleds and skis. Cars try to drive through the thick snow and get stuck. What a mess! What a lot of fun!

Winter weather: Aspects of winter weather lend themselves well to interpretation because they are action-packed and full of change. They can be done individually, in partners, or in groups. In addition to the projects given in snowflakes, these suggestions that follow might elicit group discussion and improvisations:

- Snow melted by the sun: Children in place crouch slowly as sun rays move around them.
- Fog clouding car windows and darkening the air: Show with slow lyrical movements the fog hovering everywhere, of people groping their way through it.
- Hail, pellets of hail falling and scattering: Show the dynamic jumps and leaps that hail might feel like.

Winter sports: Here there are improvisations to do on skating, ice boating, skiing, building snowmen, and having snowball fights. Do the last improvisation in partners, one throwing and the other receiving, both exaggerating the movements in slow motion. Stand far enough apart for room to really swing. Those on the receiving end should reveal exactly where they were hit, whirling and bending and then retaliating.

Improvisations on winter sports can be done in groups with each group making the other guess which sport they are doing. Note: The story "A Smile in the Snow" in Part V uses many aspects of winter.

15 Improvisations on the Visual Arts

The arts in their exquisite variations awaken our sensitivity to the world within and around us. There exist many ways to appreciate the arts through readings, lectures, performances, and active participation. This last is most fortunate for the talented and persevering among us. How privileged are we then, not as artists but through creative movement improvisations to have this way to bring the arts closer through the movement of our bodies.

Drawing

Designs: The children are given paper and pencils and are asked to draw an interesting composition using only lines. The lines should both relate and contrast with one another in thickness and direction. Naturally the older the group is, the more formal will be the results. The object will be to transpose these two-dimensional lines to movement in space. Here is a list of suggested lines:

Curved, zigzag, straight, spirals, dots, twists, circles, dashes, thin or thick, jagged.

When the drawings are completed and signed, they are propped up to enable everyone to see them. Then each child in turn tries to relate the design of the picture to movements on the floor. There is rarely any timidity about exposing one's drawing to the group, but if any exists, the works

DOI: 10.4324/9781003254812-19

can be displayed unsigned. There are several variations on this project, each of which adds other dimensions:

1. The drawings can be exchanged, allowing one child to interpret another child's drawing.
2. Two children can plan a drawing together, deciding how two lines can interrelate to make balance and design. They might begin their interpretation on opposite sides of the room and plan to weave in various ways around each other, join hands, and separate according to the patterns they have chosen.
3. A group of children can work together, one child interpreting all the straight lines, another the curving lines, another the dots, and so on.
4. Several drawings can be interpreted simultaneously.
5. Using unsigned drawings, the children can be asked to guess which design is being interpreted (A or G).

A look out the window: Look out of the window and notice how nature (as an artist) has interplayed the lines and shapes. Notice the trees especially, and the lines as tree tops meet the sky. The designs are sometimes simple, sometimes quite complex.

In the city, a look out of the window reveals buildings, vehicles, sidewalks, and roads. Notice how these structures line up against the sky above and the roads below, and the shapes and patterns that are formed. Discuss the considerations of line and balance architects must keep in mind when they plan a building. If there is a monument in view, discuss how the artist planned its lines to fit in with the surrounding landscape. If there are flower beds or shrubbery, notice how their line and design were planned. Pictures can be shown to help illustrate this. After studying the landscape, the children divide into partners or groups and plan an improvisation. They should try to make contrasts within their composition; for example, one child might interpret the tall lines of a tree while another moves in front of her as the low, horizontal ripples of water. They might announce their composition, "A tree by a lake." Their ideas may be taken directly from

Figure 15.1 Designs: Children can work together, one child interpreting all the straight lines, another the curves,
another the dots, and so on.

Credit line: Courtesy of Alice Teirstein.

what they have observed from the window, or their ideas may
be created from imagination (A or G).

Pictures come to life: The leader makes (or brings) simple
drawings of familiar animals, such as kittens, rabbits, puppies, or
lions; or people, such as clowns, police officers, fire fighters, ballet dancers, boxers, baseball players, and so forth (suggestions
can come from the children). The children, alone or in small
groups, are called on to make one of the drawings come to life.

Begin by striking the pose in the drawing then move the
way you imagine the figure would move if it were alive. Exaggerate everything as in pantomime. End the interpretation
by returning to the original pose.

This project can be varied with older children by having them draw their own rudimentary picture. In this case, the whole group interprets one child's drawing, then goes on to another, and so on.

Another variation is to turn a drawing face down and interpret it. The others then guess what is represented (A or G).

Illustrations from memory: The children describe a story they have read or has been told to them or something interesting they have recently observed or an event that they look forward to. Individually, in partners or in groups, the story images are interpreted through movement.

It is helpful to glance at some book illustrations to show how artists render ideas in a story. The children in groups can be given an *assignment* in much the same way as an illustrator is given one. That is, make a picture (a pose) to illustrate a scene in a story, referring to its characters, plot, and action. It will be interesting to note the variety of approaches to the same subject.

Painting

Colors: Seated in a wide circle, the children represent an artist's palette, each signifying a color. We will not know which one until the child responds to the artist's brush. The leader is the artist who points to each child in turn with an imaginary brush (first having assigned the colors). The child then announces a color and proceeds to move.

Colors have personal connotations, so any are perfectly appropriate. To aid in launching the project some familiar interpretations along with those that have been suggested by children follow, but **a discussion about colors and the children's own ideas and interpretations must precede this project:**

- *black:* a dark, mysterious color; the color of deep holes, nighttime (low movements, reaching, searching arms)
- *brown:* a strong color, the color of earth and trees (strong working movements)

- *blue:* a wide, soft color; the color of the sky and ocean (lyrical and flowing)
- *green:* a growing color, the color of grass, leaves, and plants, traffic go lights (forward movements and from low to high)
- *red:* a vivid, snappy color; the color of traffic stop lights, roses (jumps, leaps, skips, and hops)
- *yellow:* a bright color, the color of the sun, fire, tangy lemons (turns and high stretches)
- *white:* a soft, quiet color; the color of clouds, soap flakes, snow, lambs (delicate movements; round, curving arms)
- *pink:* a sweet, fun color; the color of babies, parties, candy (turns and running movements)
- *purple:* a royal, slightly mysterious color; the color of a king's robe, violets, sunsets (broad motions, wide turns, marching, leaping).
- *orange:* a loud, bright color; the color of pumpkins and blazing fire (jumps high in the air, flashing arms, changing head directions)

Announce to everyone the color you were assigned. Think about your feeling about the color and the things you know that are in that color. Then move in ways the color feels to you. You have your arms, hands, legs, feet, head, and whole body to splash the color across the room.

A visit to the museum: If possible, an art book with many reproductions should be procured from the library or downloaded from a museum site. The leader selects in advance the pictures that lend themselves to interpretation. Flemish and Dutch paintings (those by the Brueghels, Steen, DeHooch, Hals, and others) use lively subject matter, often humorous. Impressionist paintings (those of Sisley, Pissarro, Monet, and Seurat) inspire wistful and lyrical interpretations of people and landscapes. The gowns and bonnets worn by the women also inspire movement. Little girls love to dance Degas' scenes of the ballet, and children can bring sensitivity to Rembrandt's shadowy portraits.

Use this link to access the Metropolitan Museum of Art's access program to works in their collection: **www.metmuseum. org/art/collection. The "open access" artworks are free to print out and use.** To get you started on your museum visit, here are three artworks with suggestions about ways to bring them to life, followed by a few more artworks from which to choose:

Jan Steen's *Merry Company on a Terrace*: Many expressive movement possibilities can be seen here:

- a mandolin player
- singers and revelers

Figure 15.2 Merry Company on a Terrace, Jan Steen, Dutch, oil on canvas, 55 1/2" × 51 3/4". The Metropolitan Museum of Art, Fletcher Fund, 1958.

Credit line: Courtesy of Metropolitan Museum of Art.

- a granny with a baby
- laughing men and women
- a child playing with a dog
- the dog
- the bird that has flown out of its cage
- the toy pony
- the flute player

Exaggerate all your movements; for example, bend your torso and expansively move your arms to interpret laughter or rock your arms and dance to interpret the granny holding and singing to the baby. The musicians would move to show how they play their instruments as well as the lilt of the music they are making.

There is much to bring to life in *The Harvesters*: the trees for one, looming high over the people and spread wide in the valley below the hills. Some folks are busy harvesting

Figure 15.3 The Harvesters, 1565, Pieter Bruegel the Elder (Netherlandish, 1525–1569). Oil on wood Overall, 46 7/8 × 63 3/4 in. The Metropolitan Museum of Art. Rogers Fund, 1919.

Credit line: Courtesy of Metropolitan Museum of Art.

Figure 15.4 Self Portrait. Rembrandt van Rijn 1660. (Dutch, Leiden, 1606–1669) Oil on canvas 31 5/8 × 26 1/2 in. The Metropolitan Museum of Art. Bequest of Benjamin Altman.

Credit line: Courtesy of Metropolitan Museum of Art.

the fields while one goes to sleep under the tree. And men, women, and children eat and drink, all wearing hats under the bright sun. Exaggerate all movements and make a dance of the work in the fields.

In the discussion preceding the painting of Rembrandt's self-portrait, try to think what kind of person the figure in

Figure 15.5 At the Circus: The Spanish Walk 1899. Henri de Toulous-
         Lautrec, French, 1864–1901. Graphite, black, and
         colored pastel and charcoal, 13 3/4 × 9 13/16 in. The
         Metropolitan Museum of Art, Robert Lehman Collec-
         tion, 1975.

Credit line: Courtesy of Metropolitan Museum of Art.

Figure 15.6 Reading the News at the Weavers' Cottage 1673. Adriaen
van Ostade Dutch 1625–1685 Pen and brown ink,
watercolor, graphite, 9 5/8 × 7 15/16 in. Metropolitan Museum of Art. Bequest of Lore Heinemann, in
memory of her husband, Dr. Rudolf J. Heinemann.

Credit line: Courtesy of Metropolitan Museum of Art.

the portrait might be. What might he need or want? Begin
your interpretation of the picture in the pose Rembrandt
gives his subject. Here he stares at the artist (himself) seem-
ingly unhappy with what he sees—signs of aging perhaps

Figure 15.7 The Spanish Singer 1860. Edouard Manet (French, 1832–1883). Oil on canvas 58 × 45 in.

Gift of William Church Osborn, 1949.

Credit line: Courtesy of Metropolitan Museum of Art.

or dissatisfied with the picture he is creating. Then bring him to life in your own way. You can relate your movements to apparel—his large hat and heavy coat—or his work as a painter applying paint to the canvas. End your interpretation in the original pose.

At the Circus can be improvised by imagining the high steps of a show horse trotting around a circus ring. Add the waves of the rider to the crowd, tipping his hat and happily slapping his horse, and the enthusiastic response of the observing crowd.

Here, improvisations, in addition to the mother feeding her child and the two men absorbed in their thoughts, can include the blossoming of the trees outside. The child does not have to remain eating (he can get up and play), or the mother serving, when you bring the picture to life.

The man in *The Spanish Singer* feels like dancing to his own music and surely there are unseen folks nearby who already are. His turban flares as his head moves, and his feet can't stay still. Remember, when you bring the picture to life, it becomes *your* picture. So the moves are whatever you want them to be.

A drama can be made of A Visit to A Museum as an alternative to individual interpretations of the pictures. Here is a way to proceed for that project:

> The children see all the paintings. They then divide into groups. Each group selects a picture to interpret. Within each group selections are made for parts to improvise. Note that improvisations may include objects and nature as well as people and animals.

The children arrange themselves to roughly resemble the composition of the painting and quietly wait. The leader (or another child) pretends to visit the museum. He or she enters the great hall, looks around, and approaches the first painting. Doing so, the painting comes to life. When each improvisation finishes, the children strike the original pose, and the visitor moves on to the next painting until all the paintings have been seen. The visitor then leaves the museum with great praise for the masterpieces enjoyed.

Abstract Painting

The arrangement of forms on canvas can be interpreted to correspond to patterns of movement in space.

Figure 15.8 This abstract work in digital graphics consists of an arrangement of lines and forms. Interpret the patterns you see by creating your own patterns across the room.

Credit line: Courtesy of Simon Jeruchim.

Look at several examples of abstract painting. Note such elements as the repetition of colors and contrasts in tones from dark to light in the picture. Study the shapes and forms in the picture and the movement of lines. See how diagonals, horizontals, verticals, and curves tie forms together. In groups, explore any or all the following projects:

1. Represent individual colors of a specific painting and interpret these colors through the mood and tempo you feel the picture conveys. Colorful abstracts such as those by Jackson Pollock, Paul Klee, and Wassily Kandinsky are fun for improvisation, although the list of artists is endless and every image produced unique. Abstract painting is a direct peek into someone else's imagination.

2. Interpret the predominant forms in a painting through your movements. Painters like Paul Cezanne, Georges Braque, Piet Mondrian, and Fernand Leger play with the arrangement of forms in their pictures. The art of creating movement in space is similar to the artist painting intriguing forms on canvas.

3. Attempt your own abstractions through the use of paint, magic marker, crayon, or collage materials and then interpret your pictures through movement.

An Art Class

Crayons and paper are given out. The children make individual pictures with the artistic principles offered in the illustration titled **"Comparisons."**

Use one of these principles of composition to transfer a picture on paper to movement in space. You can use more than one of the principals, one at a time or all together. Your pictures can be abstract or realistic.

Comparisons

For the Picture

Figure 15.9 Use all your paper. Add some surrounding elements to complement a small drawing in the center of the page.

Figure 15.11 Make interesting designs; vary the lines (curved, straight), and direct their movement on your paper. Add a straight base line under the figures and a curvy horizon line under the sun and continuing behind the bushy tree, like a mountain range.

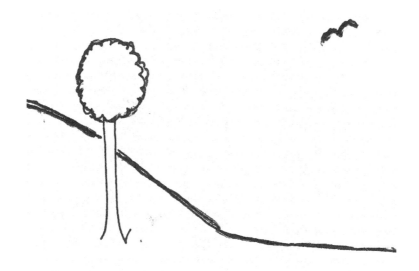

Figure 15.13 Lines can be simple but still interesting, contrasting them and using the space creatively.

For Movement in Space

Figure 15.10 Balance the stage. Busy movements in the center of the stage can begin there but then use all the space for long movements spreading out in all the corners before returning to that center at the end.

Figure 15.12 Balance the composition; many lines on one side and **few** on the other make the picture top-heavy.

Figure 15.14 Create interesting movement patterns. Contrast levels (high, low) and directions (forward, backward, circular).

Sculpture

Sculptures are predominantly three-dimensional in form, just as is the human body. Correlating sculpture to movement improvisations presents an opportunity to experience sculpture in a uniquely personal way. Any or all of the following projects offers a way to provide this experience. The project should start out with a pictorial display of sculptures and a discussion about the forms, shapes, and content. A drum on hand is an asset in performing these projects, but if not available, the leader's taps on a table will do.

Statues: Tap or drum in rhythmic three-quarter time beats: **One**-two-three, **one**-two-three, **hold**-two-three. This beat accompanies the children as they stride across the floor and then **hold** with a strong sculptural pose (the statue). Form a pose that is balanced and dynamic, which means an interesting three-dimensional design held in space, just as a good statue is.

Figure 15.15 Figure 3, Judith Peck, bronze, 24" × 18".

Repeat the sequence, each time with a different pose. Come out of the pose in a flowing manner. The "hold time" can be as long as the leader decides. Coming out can become a sequence of many small, flowing movements, as if the sculptures have come to life.

Freeze: This project can be varied in many ways. The leader can simply say, "Freeze!" as the children move about the room, and they must immediately become a statue. The project can be done in partners for more inventiveness or even in groups for more fun. In each situation, the project should be preceded by a display of sculpture and sculptural compositions inspiring children to project elements of good design into their poses.

Clay forms: Music, recorded, taped, or improvised, represents the sculptor, and the children represent mounds of clay. As the music inspires them, the children move their bodies into sculptural forms. They return as often as they like to the mound form (bent over as if in a ball) and then stretch themselves again in other ways to make new shapes.

Mobiles: After a discussion about the design of mobiles and a revue of a few images of these, the children are divided into groups; four to six in each group works well. Each set of children then tries to form a mobile, moving slowly, interweaving on high, low, or in-between planes. A variation of this project is to have some children represent the mobile, while others are the currents of air causing the mobile to move. This would be a good time to introduce the work of sculptor Alexander Calder.

Photography

The leader and the children bring in photographs from magazines or other sources. The pictures should relate to human experience, the natural world, and aspects of life that might be intriguing to interpret. *National* Geographic lends itself ideally to this project. Also, the *Family of Man* album contains photographs of people that are inspiring and provide good material to stimulate the imagination. This project can be done either by directly interpreting the photograph or by using the photograph simply as a beginning idea to further explore through movement. Both the leader and children may have photographs they themselves have taken, stored on their smartphones, and these should be explored as well.

16 Improvisations on the Performing Arts

Music

Rhythm band: Sitting in a circle on the floor, the leader selects a student to beat the drum in a steady two-quarter beat (dum dum, dum dum). The group, as a whole, first copies the beat and then begins to improvise rhythms by clapping or tapping on a book or table to add to the dominant beat. When the group is warmed up—groovy so to speak—the project ends, or children can take turns leading the group with a beat they are asked to follow.

An example of a steady two-quarter beat with variations is as follows:

- Steady beat: dum dum dum dum
- Variation: dum da-da-da dum, da-da-da dum, da-da-da dum
- Or simply: dum da-da, dum da-da, dum da-da, dum da-da
- Or another variation: da-da-da-da dum, da-da-da-da dum, da-da-da-da dum, da-da-da da dum

Ideally there should be at least two drums: one for a student who maintains a loud steady tempo and the other for the leader's use to emphasize each of the children's improvisations so that the others will be able to repeat it. While the rhythms are more fun when instruments are available, they can easily be done by clapping hands together or on the knees or on a desk or on the floor.

Rhythm dances: This project can follow the preceding one. Each time new rhythms are created, a child goes to the middle

DOI: 10.4324/9781003254812-20

of the circle and improvises a dance or series of movements to fit. The children outside the circle clap or beat something for accompaniment either in the basic beat or new one. The child in the middle selects another child to replace her. The rhythms also can change, originating from different children. In this way, all members of the group have a chance to either dance or compose a rhythm.

Sounds: Sitting in a circle on the floor, each child suggests an idea, for example, a motorcycle starting up and driving off. The child then improvises a corresponding rhythmic sound with his voice, such as VRUMMM VRUMMM VRUMMM or with a drum. The others join in to make their own improvisations on this theme. Then all those who wish stand up and interpret the idea with movement, while the others continue the sounds. Some examples of things that make interesting sounds are these:

- a train going into or out of a station
- a ball bouncing
- wind becoming a storm
- stamping on crisp leaves or bubble wrap
- rush hour traffic

For variation, one child can be the conductor, indicating with a pretend baton when the sound and the movement should be fast, slow, or when they should start and stop. The children observe and follow the directions (A or G).

Orchestra: The class is divided into three sections for an orchestral work we will title "Storm"; one child is chosen as the conductor and stands while the other two groups sit or stand in a circle watching the conductor to know when to start, stop, increase or decrease their tempo. For example, *Section 1* might their rub feet along the floor, making sounds like *wind. Section 2 might* patter their feet like soft rain. The conductor indicates an increase in tempo, and *Sections 1* and *2* increase their movements in sound and fury. Both sections might shout out or pound a drum for *lightning* sounds and thunder.

It is a good idea to begin the orchestra project with a simple theme like this. Then leaders and groups can plan other themes to orchestrate. After the "performance," the leader could have a discussion on how real orchestras operate and perhaps play a well-chosen musical tape.

Forms of music—for older children: The leader and children discuss different forms of music; perhaps tapes are played of some varieties. Afterward, groups are formed and each group selects one type of music to interpret. Some suitable areas are:

- folk music
- orchestral music
- jazz
- opera
- disco, rap, popular vocal

Solo instruments such as piano, flute, harp, violin, cello, trumpet, percussion, and voice can be described and discussed. These would be challenging to interpret in movement, but with the right recording revealing the sound of individual instruments, it could be delightful.

Musical stories: Many stories and activities for children with musical accompaniment are available. Some are adaptable for interpretive movement and some are not. Look for those with story content active enough *for* improvisation and musical background *of* good quality. The leader is free to wield the *needle* unmercifully, eliminating passages that are weak, using only a portion of the music, or fading it out to end somewhere in the middle. Here are two examples of recorded stories that can be adapted for creative movement improvisations:

- *Tubby the Tuba:* Play it through first, then discuss the instruments and improvise creative movements for them. After this, choose parts then play it again with each child moving at the appropriate time in the story. The story should be interpreted several times to get the most out of its musical content. *Tubby the Tuba* makes a good project to rehearse and present to an audience.

- *Peter and the Wolf* (Prokofiev): Play the tape through; discuss it; then play it again. The children choose the part they want to be and *enter the scene* when the story indicates, interpreting their character however they wish. Determine ahead of time where the tree and other locales would be in the room.

Additional recordings are listed among the sources at the end of the book, but keep in mind that these are merely suggestions. Virtually any musical story with implied action has creative movement potential.

Drama

Pantomime

Pantomime involves movement only, not speech, and is an exaggeration of natural gestures. To practice pantomime, develop ordinary hand gestures into movements of the whole body.

- Mime "come here" to one person at a time making the movement as big as possible.
- Mime "come here" collectively to everyone and see how that changes the movement.
- Call someone down from a ladder to you high above.
- Call a kitten hiding under the bed to you.

Other strong gestures for pantomime, which can also be expanded on high and low planes, are:

- "Go away!" It can be done impatiently.
- "This is for you." Pretend to give things to this person or that one. Expand the gesture by waving to someone upstairs. Then scatter seeds along the ground.
- "Whoops! I dropped it!" Your arms fly up in exasperation.
- "I'll pick it up." Show how the object is a strain to manage or cumbersome or light as a feather or slippery or wet or a tender bundle like a baby.

Discuss a range of ideas you might show in pantomime. Common themes such as walking to school and greeting others, shopping for food with a parent, playing sports, going on vacation, taking care of younger children, and doing tasks like hauling out the garbage make for good pantomimes. In addition to becoming better at improvising moves, you become more aware of these ordinary activities that you are seeing and doing after they are pantomimed.

Add to the project by asking others to guess the pantomime themes. Remember, the more movements are exaggerated, the easier they are to be guessed correctly.

Groups can also make up stories based on a single pantomime. For example, using the gesture "This is for you," make up a story about an old woman who goes to the park every day to feed the birds. The story can develop, have a plot, interesting characters, other scenes, and so on. One can go as far as time permits with this project. It is a good way of combining story with movement and pantomime (A or G).

Emotions

In a group discussion, express emotions familiar to everyone such as feeling sad, feeling joyful, feeling afraid, feeling strong, feeling stupid. Describe incidents in which these emotions were experienced. Then show ways these emotions can be described in movements.

Words that excite emotional reactions can also be interpreted in this manner. Some suggestions follow:

weakness	fear	happiness
timidity	tough	sadness
silliness	anger	mean
shyness	hurt	foolish
loving	hate	dumb

Stories

Familiar children's stories can be dramatized through creative movement: excerpts from classics such as *Huckleberry Finn*; fairy tales with a lot of action like *Cinderella, Jack and the Beanstalk, Hansel and Gretel, Sleeping Beauty, Rumpelstiltskin,*

and *Snow White*, as well as contemporary juvenile fiction and picture books. The procedure is similar to other projects:
  Groups meet together and discuss stories they know.

A story is chosen.
Parts are selected.
An announcer introduces the scene and the characters.
A pose is struck, and the story begins.

Figure 16.1 Hansel and Gretel, lost in the forest. Gretel is worried as night falls and Hansel comforts her. (Camper at Camp Chateaugay and Sabrina Peck, Merrill, NY)

The announcer can narrate as the creative movement story is performed or the story done with only musical accompaniment. Music can be any selection that seems to fit the general mood. Debussy's piano music complements many stories. The dramatization can be done in one group, the leader reading the story and then giving out parts without asking the children to select their own. Otherwise, a group might find itself with twelve Sleeping Beauties. The procedure will vary with the available facilities and the age and temperament of the group (A or G).

Original stories: The leader offers subject matter for a topic. A discussion follows, after which the children divide

Figure 16.2 The witch has put Hansel in the oven and Gretel cries out, seeing him there. (Campers at Camp Chateaugay, Merrill, NY)

into groups and make up stories related to the topic. Some provocative subject areas might be the following:

good deeds
mischief
insects and animals
the four seasons
sports
holidays
famous people
other countries
after-school activities
vehicles
exotic environments such as jungles, deserts, mountains,
   the sea

Poems: A.A. Milne, Dr. Seuss, Longfellow, Ogden Nash, and other poets provide good material for improvisation. Again remember that flowers, rain, sun, trees, moon, wind, snow, and other elements are all parts that can be interpreted.

Songs: Nursery rhymes, holiday songs, folk songs, and ballads can be dramatized through interpretive movement.

Puppet shows: The children make up a simple story and present it as if they were puppets. One child can tell the story as it is being enacted by the puppets. The story can be little more than an idea, for example, a Punch and Judy type with two people fighting and making up. Or it can represent animal puppets or circus performers going about their respective activities. Imaginary admission tickets should be asked for just before the show to add an air of importance (A or G).

Words: The leader chooses a word, and all the children together express what the word means to them by their improvisations or pantomime. If a source of music is available—a piano or drum for example—the music can be improvised to suit the nature of the word.

As a variation children can supply the word to be interpreted. Some words that produce interesting reactions include the following:

mother	sister	universe
father	brother	grandfather
baby	friend	grandmother
me	police officer	teacher
cowboy	dancer	principal
traffic	trucks	farmer
the president	nuclear power	

Verbs and adjectives, as well as nouns, can be used. The leader's own imagination can run riot here and when the children have their turn to supply words, they can also have free rein. Each word should be delivered strongly, allowing a short interval for interpretation before going on to the next.

17 Improvisations on the Holidays

Holidays in their actual functioning encompass more than the honoring of a person or event. There is a sense of celebration, of something special in the day; children might have a day off from school and adults from work. Signs of the festivities will appear in news media or on the streets. People will, by necessity, experience the special day in different ways. But *experiencing* it is what we do. And the ways in which we do this serve to bring us closer to one another. A few common holidays, enjoyed by children particularly, and some movement projects to accompany them are offered here.

Easter

Easter eggs: The following story should be interpreted in one group. One child, with a flourish and exaggerated movements, *paints* a basket of Easter eggs in various colors and patterns, such as stripes, polka dots, zigzags, squiggles, and circles. Other children, in the role of the *eggs*, interpret the color or design they are being painted; the painter then summons each egg one at a time to a place somewhere in the room to hide.

Two other children enter and begin their Easter egg hunt, searching *high* and *low*. They find the *eggs* and *lead* them to their *baskets*. At the end of this search and discover, the painter and the children pretend to lift their baskets. But oh my! The *baskets* drop! The *eggs* jiggle around, they scatter and tumble about, and some crack open. Altogether, everyone emerges as the children they really are and take a bow (to the leader's resounding applause).

DOI: 10.4324/9781003254812-21

Easter chicks and rabbits: If young children are asked to make up a story about Easter, in all probability, they will want to include chicks or bunnies. Using picture books that show rabbits and baby chicks provides an easy path for these improvisations. Distribute the various parts contained in the story to make it come alive. Remember to include the surrounding elements for improvisation if it adds to the telling.

Halloween

Halloween costumes: Improvisations on the characters represented by Halloween costumes can be done in a variety of ways:

1. Children bring the costumes they intend to wear for "trick or treating" and move as the characters would move. These interpretations must be preceded by a thoughtful group discussion about the characters represented. Do this by inventing various scenarios they might react to. (Masks may or may not be used.)
2. The leader pretends to pull a heavy box into the center of the room and then presents each child with a costume, whispering in the child's ear what kind of costume it is. The children go off to a corner and pretend to dress; then each child interprets the character he or she represents while the others try to guess. Costumes need not relate to Halloween. They may also be accessories of an interesting nature, such as ballet tutu, Spanish fan, clown outfit, flower basket, cowboy lasso, queen's robe and crown, space suit, boxing gloves, Batman mask, lion tamer's whip, hiker's backpack, king's robe and crown, doctor's stethoscope, Superman cape, baseball suit, Spiderman outfit, and suggestions by the children themselves.
3. In groups, the children make up short stories about Halloween characters and create the moves to act them out. For example, a skeleton, a princess, and a black cat could combine to make a most sinister tale. This variation can also be used should the children arrive in actual costumes. Voices can be added for the spooky fun of it.

Thanksgiving

Thanksgiving: The first thing that comes to a child's mind about this holiday is the turkey dinner, but there are limitations to the creative potential of sweet potatoes and stuffing. Older children can create improvisations around the theme of Thanksgiving, for example, different stages in the Pilgrims' arrival: the crossing on the *Mayflower*, encountering the Native Americans, planting corn, the hardships, and the giving thanks. Natural elements, such as rain, cold weather, storms, and fire, should be used in these interpretations.

Christmas

Christmas toys: Improvisations on this theme are varied and abundant:

1. The children tell what they would like to receive for Christmas, then interpret these items either individually or in groups (A or G).
2. After Christmas, the children show by improvisations what they received (A or G).
3. All the children but one represent various toys and presents and curl up under a make-believe tree. The other child pretends to wake up on Christmas Day and then runs to the tree to see what presents are there and unwraps them one by one. The presents improvise according to what they represent and are then put back under the tree. For the finale, the child *picks up* all the presents and plays with them as everyone moves "nimbly and merrily" around the room.
4. The children line up as toys in a toy store. A storekeeper fusses over them, dusting and arranging them until a customer comes into the shop. She looks the toys over carefully and finally points to one. The storekeeper pulls the toy forward and *winds it up*; the toy improvises according to what it represents. The customer sighs indecisively and points to another. Again the storekeeper pulls it forward. The process continues until all the toys have done an improvisation after which the customer either chooses

one or decides to take them all. She pays the shopkeeper, and the toys follow her out. *(In the event that she buys them all, she should ask to have them sent.)*

5. Creating and building toys is shown by exaggerated motions of hammering, sawing, painting, manipulating keys on a computer and other aspects of toy and game fabrication. Some children can be the craftspeople and some, the objects being worked on such as puppets, wagons, dolls, sports balls, stuffed animals, robots, Nintendo, and other digital action games.

Christmas stories: Illustrated picture books featuring Santa Claus, the reindeer, and other topics relating to this holiday season, both in the human and animal realm, make good material for creative movement. The story is read, parts are chosen, and the play is presented as the leader narrates.

Christmas trees: Interpret the decorations used for Christmas trees, such as tinsel, bells, lights, stars, and angels. Think of the feel of these decorations, the shapes they take, their textures, and how they sound. Several children can represent each type of ornament: entering, improvising, and then placing themselves high or low along the imaginary branches of a tree. One child can be the decorator, bringing in and attaching the ornaments high, low, and every which way. The leader can flip a switch when the tree is ready to light, and the ornaments can "light up" as they please.

Christmas cards: The leader brings to class selected Christmas cards with scenes of people, animals, wintery landscapes, sleighs, Santa, and warm hearths, and the children make the illustrations come to life. New stories can be created with ideas suggested by the scenes and presented as movement plays.

Christmas spirit: Interpret facets of human relationships such as sharing the gifts you've been given, love of others, caring for people in need whom you may not even know, friendships (including the feeling of being left out). Each group should make up and present a short movement play as an example of one or more of these ideas (*G*).

Other Festivities
New Year's resolutions: Discuss worthwhile New Year's resolutions and demonstrate them through movement exaggerations while the other children try to guess what they are. Suggestions include the following:

- helping with chores
- taking good care of teeth
- getting places on time
- spending less time talking on the phone and texting
- keeping room neat
- working more on homework/reading/listening

Religious holidays: This project would be done in religious schools as opposed to other public and private school settings. Characters and significant events can be dramatized in movement and pantomime, following procedures already described. Here are a few holidays that might be enriched in meaning by movement interpretations:

Advent
Palm Sunday
Pentecost
Rosh Hashanah
Yom Kippur
Sukkoth
Passover
Shavuoth
Ramadan

Hanukkah dreidels: The dreidel, a small colorful top that spins, is easily interpreted in movement by various color patterns and changing speeds, from fast to slow. As the dreidel slows down, it tilts precariously in many directions before finally *falling down*. The dreidel's turns, sways, waddles, and slow collapse lend themselves to lots of creative moves. Done in a group, the dreidel's upset and collapse can make for a cheerful combination of creative movement and fun.
Other holidays to consider

Figure 17.1 Dancers improvise to make dreams appear to come alive as others watch, interpreting what they see.

Credit line: Courtesy of CityStep.

Ethnic celebrations: Festivals that various ethnic groups enjoy, for example, the Chinese New Year, are described by individuals to others in the group, after which the festival is interpreted together. Articles or artifacts used in the celebrations can be brought in to enhance the descriptions.

Preparation for a holiday makes lively material for improvisation, not only the doing by day but also the dreaming by night. Put these thoughts and stories into action.

18 School Projects

The subject matter in this endeavor is understandably expansive as improvisations might relate to literature and taking dramatic ideas from fiction, or geography inspired by its diversity of people, culture and sights, or science with its experiments and advances, or history involving its prominent people and events. The discussion at the start of the project should encourage children to bring any subject matter they are interested in exploring to the table.

Letters in names: The children use their bodies to form the shapes of letters appearing in their names. The design of each letter can be made while standing in place or moving. All movements are exaggerated and the whole body is used, not only hands or arms. Ideas may be based on block letters or on script. Then each child selects the name of someone else in the room and forms the letters of that person's name. The other children must guess whose name it is (*G*).

Handwriting: Interpret the kinds of writing that are being learned or have already been learned by forming movements for the predominant rhythm and design of each. Some examples with suggested movements are as follows:

- *Capital letters:* broad square movements, high jumps, and wide turns
- *Print:* smaller motions, precise and staccato
- *Script:* lyrical, connected, fluid movements—dot the *i*'s with jumps
- *Punctuation marks:* exclamation point—stretch and jump; question mark—curve and jump; periods—little jumps,

DOI: 10.4324/9781003254812-22

skips, or hops; commas—curves and half-turns; dashes—
long stretches to the side

Science experiments: The science corner in most classrooms is usually full of interesting material that can be interpreted. Experiments about the growth and care of plants,
insects, and animals; the processes of change taking place
in nature around us; and experiments with rocks, miner-
als, and chemicals are only a few of the subjects that can be
explored. Physical interpretation of these experiments may
increase the child's interest and understanding since it is a
way of participating in the transformations observed.

Geography: After a discussion of some geographic points
of interest on the map of the United States, the children
individually decide what part of the country they would like
to interpret. They arrange themselves across the room to be
in the approximate location of each point's situation on the
map. For example, Florida would be toward the front on the
right side of the room, and the Great Lakes would be toward
the back and to the right of center. As the leader mentions
characteristic sights and important facts about each locale,
the children representing that part of the country interpret
the descriptions. Some popular areas include the following:

New York City
Cape Cod
Hollywood
Florida
Mississippi River
Great Lakes
Yellowstone Park
San Francisco
Pacific and Atlantic Ocean
Texas
Niagara Falls

History: Choose a specific study under discussion in your
classes. Discuss under the leader's guidance some of the
principal facts involved. Think about how you might see

the actions happening in your mind's eye and share these if you choose to. Then in groups, select at least one feature of special interest to you about the characters, events, or scenes in the episode. Plan together a brief creative movement play to portray the scene. Choose parts and experiment with moves depicting actions that bring the episode to life. Present the story to other groups while the leader narrates. (*Note:* "The History Class" in Part V is a story relating to this project.)

Library: In groups, children decide on particular fiction books, stories, or poems to interpret. They choose parts and wait in a corner of the room. A child enters, pretending to be in a library. The child selects a book from the shelf, announces the title, and begins to read. As the child thinks about the story, it comes to life. Each group interprets its chosen story through movement and then returns to the corner. The same process is repeated for every story. Current classroom studies can be used in this project in place of fiction.

Current events: Items of interest that the children have observed on television, seen online, heard on the radio, or read in print are interpreted in a manner similar to that used in the project "Library." Groups of children select their subject and wait. A child pretends to open a magazine and then mentions an item of interest; it is interpreted. News items with an element of action are the most suitable, such as the space program, blizzards, floods and tornados, circus and zoo events, sports announcements, even the funny papers. Children can be asked to look for articles and collect them for the project.

Prominent people: Significant facts in the lives of people who have made special contributions to our culture, our country, and the quality of our lives are interpreted. Interesting categories would include the following:

- political and public leaders (Martin Luther King, Eleanor Roosevelt, etc.)
- musicians and conductors (Vladimir Horowitz, Leonard Bernstein, etc.)

- painters and sculptors (Pablo Picasso, Michelangelo, etc.)
- dancers (Isadora Duncan, Martha Graham, etc.)
- scientists (Albert Einstein, Covid vaccine researchers, etc.)
- social scientists (Albert Schweitzer, etc.)
- sports figures, actors, writers, teachers, health care experts, and others

Great books in action: This is a chance to share beloved classic books. The leader provides a brief summary of their favorites, describing the characters and the plot. A passage from the book is read aloud by the leader (or by the children if for a purposeful objective). The leader summons movement interpretations by the group at prudent sections. The children stand to bring the incident to life and then sit again to hear more of the story. This project is best done together as one group throughout, sitting comfortably in a circle on the floor or chairs as the leader reads and summons the interpretations. This is because the story may be too gripping to leave to form separate groups. In a religious setting, portions of the Bible as history, drama, or ritual can be read and interpreted in this way.

19 Fun and Games

As in several of the other projects described, the geographic communities in which children live will determine ideas in terms of where and what their entertainments come from. After doing one or two of the improvisations, children might be asked to name what idea of their own they'd like the group to improvise.

Fishing: Some children work as fishermen throwing out their imaginary lines. Other children are *fish*: strong ones fighting the line, others gliding into it on the waves, and others jumping in the air before being caught. The *fish* swim about, get caught on the fishermen's lines, and are pulled in. Show the tension on each line: the fisherman *pull*, and the *fish* are *pulled*. There is such intensity in that pull that the line between them appears to be real. Parts are changed afterward, which is fair enough, although far from realistic. At the end, the *fish* are tossed back into the water to swim again, and the fishermen go home with poles on their shoulders and pails under their arms, satisfied with their catch and kindly actions.

Camping: Setting up the tent and then foraging for wood to make a fire is action enough for a story given what you might find in the woods. But the plot thickens when a big black bear shows up when you are preparing the food over the fire. Lots of parts to take in on such an outing.

A trip to New York City: What you could see and do on a visit to the big city makes for lively topics to discuss and then

DOI: 10.4324/9781003254812-23

interpret. The leader pretends to take a bus ride through the city, getting off at different points of interest. Meanwhile, the children crouch low at various places around the room waiting to represent the things the leader will discover (!). They rise to become the sight, sound, content, and/or activity of that sight. Suggested sights follow:

- museums (paintings, sculptures, drawings, jewels, artifacts, ceramics)
- playgrounds and parks (swings, seesaws, joggers, cyclists, nannies, and moms pushing baby strollers and chatting)
- concerts—each child can be a musical instrument and one the conductor
- tall buildings
- steam shovels, bulldozers, and derricks
- subways, buses, trucks, taxis, and motorcycles
- people, dressed fancy and plain
- dogs, squirrels, and pigeons
- the zoo
- helicopters, airplanes, and skywriters
- theater and opera
- street musicians
- ships entering and leaving their piers
- police officers directing traffic, pounding a beat, riding on horses
- pretzel, chestnut, and ice cream vendors

A variation of this project is to plan stories using a combination of sights and activities and present them as movement plays.

Animal crackers: Use real or imaginary animal crackers. Each child takes or is served an animal cookie and quickly consumes it. Each child in turn then interprets the action of that animal while the others try to guess what it is. (Preschool children have been known to confound the guessers because by the time their turn comes, they have forgotten what they ate.) This is a good project for parties when cookies and punch are served.

Taffy pull: The leader gives a make-believe ball of taffy to each set of partners. Children stand apart and pull, stretch, and twist the taffy, exaggerating the pulling movements to strengthen the tension. Some add-ons might be to become twisted up in the taffy. You can substitute the idea of rubber bands for taffy.

Vehicles: In one group, explore various forms of locomotion. Movements can be interpreted kneeling in place, sitting on a chair, or standing. Or they can be done with repetitive movements across the floor. After various vehicles are discussed together, children can experiment ways in which to interpret the special movements of each and what it is affected by, for example, wind, water, air, rocky roads, and fuel. Suggested vehicles:

cars	rockets	
bikes	helicopters	submarines
	canoes	balloons
jalopies	rowboats	roller coasters
planes	sailboats	motorcycles
jets	steamships	horse and wagon

Why not end the individual interpretations of these vehicles with a giant traffic jam!

TV shows: After a thorough discussion of favorite programs, including programs suggested by the leader, the children divide into groups. Each group represents a separate channel and plans a particular program to present. These programs can be based on weekly shows the children follow or cartoons or TV "specials" such as ballets, puppet shows, circus acts, or musical comedy. The show need not have a plot but can consist of celebrities doing what they are known for.

When the plans are completed, the leader clicks a remote, pretending to select a channel while everyone except the group representing that channel sits and watches like the audience. The selected channel presents its program. (The leader and the group can pretend to walk to the fridge, eat, do exercises, shoot a basket, whatever—as you

Figure 19.1 A trip to New York City: Tall buildings with so much activity inside: concerts, theater, opera, art—and people everywhere—working, shopping, selling, rushing, eating, strolling . . .

Credit line: Photo by Erik Unhjem.

might do while watching TV.) The leader then switches to another channel and so on until all the groups have performed.

Games: Board games should make for fun action. Think of your game piece cruising around the board, stopping at a not-so-happy place, and spending the night in jail. All board

Figure 19.2 Simple movements like a run allow for ways to improvise.

Credit line: Courtesy of CityStep.

games have rewards and penalties that keep the players "on their toes." Circuitous routes and bumping into chutes and ladders can be anywhere. Even Candy Land has its pitfalls.

Part V

Creative Movement Plays

The creative movement stories are designed to support storytelling, reading, imagination, and understanding. Success in achieving their goals is not measured by the quality of performance but by the vitality of the process.

Credit line: Courtesy of Alice Teirstein.

DOI: 10.4324/9781003254812-24

20 Dynamic Plays

The stories in this section have been written by the author expressly for creative interpretation by children. They have been performed many times by children of varying ages, so in that sense are "factory tested." Some stories were improved by ideas the children contributed, and some were changed to allow more of their favorite characters to appear.

A word about characters: the stories include an assortment of imaginary characters and elements of nature. Rain, flowers, sun, wind, and stars will come alive. It is hoped that through their interpretations, the children will become more sensitive to these daily gifts that abound. Verbal discussion of the elements in the story should accompany the stories after the reading and before the improvisations.

Adapting the Stories for the Group in Session

The age range for which each story would have the most appeal is given after the title, followed by the cast of characters. These guidelines will allow you to see at a glance if the story is suited to the needs of your group. However, consider that the stories can be changed—characters changed, added to, or reduced with respect to the number of children present, their gender, the time at your disposal, the room size, and your own interests.

The stories are planned for a normal-sized room with a degree of open space to move, first to be read aloud while everyone is seated and then to proceed as described in the next section. The children, if not barefoot, should be

DOI: 10.4324/9781003254812-25

wearing comfortable shoes and dressed in regular school or play clothes.

Procedure for Preparing the Movement Play

To consider the story for your group, first read the story yourself. Then look through the *Suggestions* which are offered for adapting the stories to movement plays. If you choose to go forward, begin by reading the story aloud to the group. After that, lead a discussion on expanding the ideas presented. For example, if a spreading fire appears in the story, ask the children if they have ever seen a fire or pictures of one: what did it look like, were they frightened by it, what colors flamed in the fire, and how should they deal with a fire if it is in the wrong place. These questions project the children into the situation and, thinking about the elements involved, prepare them for the physical improvisation.

Volunteers are then asked to improvise the movement of a fire growing and spreading. If a wind is mentioned in the story, the group goes to the window (if available) and observes the wind's effect on the scenery (if there is one). The children are asked to name the things they see the wind touching. Does it move branches on trees and scatter leaves on the ground the same way? Why not? They are then asked to show with their arms, legs, torsos, necks, and heads ways in which the branches and leaves would move in a brisk wind.

Children can volunteer to show individual movements or the whole group can interpret these ideas together. Sometimes, in a large class, it is advisable to choose just a few children at a time. This not only gives each child sufficient room to move but tends to make being chosen a privilege, an attitude that works to the leader's advantage.

Next, parts are chosen, adapting the written cast of characters to fit the group, not vice versa as in a "legitimate" play. For example, there can be two winds instead of one or none at all.

Beginning the Movement Play

The characters that begin "onstage" are placed and the others are sent off to the "wings" to wait (anywhere on the sidelines). The term *stage* refers only to the area being used for the play, there most likely not being a stage in use, and the term used here only differentiates the working area from the area where children are watching and waiting. You might change the positioning of the children to have all characters on stage throughout, crouching with heads down when they are not "on." This is a useful method when the class is composed of very young or mischievous children who can be more easily kept in order in this fashion.

The title of the play is formally announced (either by you or a child) to an imaginary audience. Then when everyone is ready, you wave up an imaginary curtain and the story begins.

Your job as storyteller is far more than reading; you are, in essence, the director, sole accompaniment, and avid audience. The vitality of your expression as you read the story aloud can directly affect the quality of movement produced. Read also with pauses wherever a character needs *time* to *develop* an improvisation. This will not be indicated in the story. At the end of the story, applaud (with both hands and knees if no one else is around). Everyone then, "dead or alive," takes a bow.

Space, Sound, and Clothing as Instruments of Expression

Some words or phrases are built into the story for the purpose of expanding spatial movement: "She ran *all* about" and "They searched *all* along the floor." The combination of the words and the leader *stretching* out the phrase can work to produce a wider use of space. "From corner to corner," a description that appears frequently in the suggestions following each story, encourages the child to use all the space provided. It does not mean moving back and forth, from one side to another, but rather leaving the center to explore all four corners.

A word about words: If the writer sometimes appears emotionally manic, repeatedly using such hysterical words as *overjoyed, wonderful, magnificent, grim, horrified,* and such, it is not to convey personal reactions to given stimuli. The words are chosen, tossed overboard, in fact, like food for the seagulls, to stir children to transfer the excitement of the words to their movements.

If you are lucky enough to have piano music available, or a live pianist, the music can assist the action interpretively or simply provide background to your voice. A musical tape might be selected in advance of the presentation, choosing an overall tone in the tenor of the action. Musical selections on your smartphone may work surprisingly well, The music can be supplemented with a drum to provide special effects where needed. Children who for some reason do not want to be in the play can be given this accompaniment to perform.

In every case that costumes are described, the costumes are imaginary and for the purpose of stimulating movement. They are not to indicate what the child should be wearing. For example, if the story indicates that a Spanish doll is wearing a full lace dress and waving a fan, the description is intended to help the child create interesting and characteristic movements. She can swirl to show the full skirt and be haughty or coy with motions of her fan. These moves make the improvisation more exciting and the character more believable. For the same reason, descriptions such as "she combed her *long* hair" are given to indicate gestures that can be enlarged to create broad and clearly defined movements.

Preparing the Movement Stories as Program Entertainment

Although these stories are prepared for informal use, they can be made into programs for an audience of other children. The advantage here is that as few as three rehearsals can produce a show. The audience, moreover, will find a lot in common with the presentation: They own the instruments of expression and therefore can conceive of their own bodies doing the movements they see. They relate easily to the subject matter since the activities, images, and topics are familiar. And should you want to add this element, the audience afterward might join the leader and performers in a discussion of the subject matter similar to the way that was done originally. If the audience is small, you might bravely read the story through again with those new folks "onstage" to improvise any of the roles they choose.

You might select a story to perform by its relationship to a time of year or an event relevant to the group and audience. To further the story's appeal simple costumes or accoutrements can be devised by the leader or by the children from their own wardrobes. Finally, informal accompaniment, such as percussion instruments, audience clapping, sound effects with found objects or voice incantations can be worked into the program to add a little "oomph."

Movement Story Reminders

The procedure for adapting stories or projects for entertainment purposes is the same as the method for informal use. The creative movement play for a live audience should be rehearsed two or three times to clarify entrances and exits and to develop broader improvisations. In performing the stories, the following things should be explained (if not duly followed):

1. Beginning and ending movements or poses are important since they give the creative movement play structure and dramatic impact.
2. All action should be BIG enough for the person in the last row to see it.
3. Characters as they move should be aware of the others on stage and relate to them.
4. Once a child is *onstage,* he or she should stay in character the whole time, not "drop," stand still, or look around as an observer.

Conclusion

These stories are primarily vehicles for the children, designed to encourage their growth on many levels. The children's success in interpreting the stories cannot be measured by the quality of their movements but by the vitality of the process. Equally important, the leader's success, as in all the projects, should not be measured by the quality of the productions but by the desire of the children to do them again.

21 The Stories

Star Party
The Robin Family
The Visits
A Magic Sewing Box
The Treasure Chest
A Shoe Tree
Robert the Rabbit
A Smile in the Snow
The House on the Hill
The History Class
The Speed and Fury of Fire
A Small Statue
The Baby Bud
The Pencil Party
The New Old Woman in the Shoe

Star Party (ages 6–11)

Characters

Shooting Star
Stars
Moon
Winds
North Wind
Sun
Baby Stars

DOI: 10.4324/9781003254812-26

Star Party

Have you ever seen a star party? Perhaps you could if you are very good at imagining. Of course, the night must be clear so that you can see all the stars come out. Then if you watch the sky closely, you might be able to imagine one going on. This is the story of a star party that happened one night, high up in the sky, far from all the sleeping people below on earth.

***

The sky was very dark, and all the Stars were asleep. Suddenly, a Shooting Star raced through the sky, waking all the Stars and calling, "Star party! Star party! Her majesty the Full Moon is coming out tonight and there is going to be a party in her honor!"

Quick as a wink, the Stars jumped out of their beds and with great excitement began to dress. They donned their silver gowns, buttoned on their glistening shoes, and helped each other fasten sparkling jewels about their necks and twinkling bracelets on their arms. They threw silver dust playfully at each other until it covered their heads. Then laughing joyfully, they glided out into the sky.

There, the soft Winds had already begun to play the music and melodies filled the night. The Full Moon had risen and was seated on her glowing throne for she was Queen of the Night. Her white rays reached out to all the Stars, and they winked back at her in greeting.

Then the Stars began to dance. Some danced alone while others formed into groups, making lovely patterns in the sky. All the Stars enjoyed themselves for the music of the Winds made the party very gay.

But after a few hours passed by, the big North Wind, who was playing in the orchestra, became tired of staying in one place. He decided to stir up a little mischief. While the other Winds were playing a lively polka, he roused himself and began to wander among the dancing Stars. In and out of the Star clusters he blew, upsetting their patterns and making a big nuisance of himself.

"Go back to the orchestra," called the Stars. "Use your powerful breath to make music. You are upsetting our dances!"

But the North Wind paid no attention. He was having fun. Just then he spied a group of Baby Stars playing along the Milky Way. There, a long white table had been spread with many dainties, dips, and delicacies for the Stars. The Baby Stars were sharing a dipper of dewdrops when the North Wind came upon them. "Like to go for a little ride?" the North Wind asked with a sly grin. Without waiting for an answer, he swept all of them into his strong arms at once. Down the Milky Way they sailed. Faster and faster! When they reached the end, the North Wind turned around and sped them even faster back again to where they started. Then off he raced once more, down the Milky Way, with the laughing Baby Stars held tightly in his arms.

The older Stars saw what was happening and quickly gathered along the Milky Way. They were worried about the Baby Stars even though the little ones could be heard all through the sky laughing gleefully. The older Stars called to the North Wind to stop, but he paid no attention. Finally, some of them approached the Queen and asked her to make the North Wind behave himself. The Queen Moon stood and cast a ray in the direction of the North Wind. He saw it at once and without delay, he slowed his speed, placed the Baby Stars down, and went obediently back to his place in the orchestra.

The Winds continued to play all night long. The Stars danced and frolicked, and the sky was aglow with the glorious party. Then, suddenly the Shooting Star raced anxiously among the Stars and called, "To sleep, to sleep, her Majesty the Sun is coming, and we must make way!"

Sure enough, the Stars looked down and could already see the crimson chariot heralding the Sun's arrival. They said goodnight to the Moon, and off they went, back to their cloud beds. There, all talking and twinkling at once about the exciting party and the mischievous North Wind, the Stars helped each other off with their gowns, slippers, and jewels. Then, with tired toes and sleepy sighs, they closed their eyes and went to sleep.

The Moon waited for a little while alone in the sky. The Sun was coming nearer now. The red chariot had left her at the horizon, and she was rising alone, bringing with her the light of day. At last the Sun was near enough for the Moon to greet: "My night is ended, and your day begins," she called. "You will bring cheer to the people on Earth, I know." Slowly, the beautiful Moon disappeared, and the Sun placed herself upon the throne. Now the sky held a new queen, the brilliant Queen of Daylight.

The happy party had ended, but the Stars talked about it for many nights afterward as they twinkled together in the sky.

Suggestions

Note that the genders indicated are arbitrary in performing the story. In the preparatory discussion, encourage children to compare what they have seen in the night sky, such as the stars, moon, and rising sun, to aspects of this make-believe story. Ask if they have ever seen a shooting star or the Milky Way or the sun and the moon together in the sky. Bringing in pictures of the night sky could be helpful. Ask if they could imagine a star party in the sky.

The stars are lying on half the stage toward one side when the shooting star darts in with zigzag runs and leaps. He moves around the stars, and they awaken.

When the stars put on their gowns and jewels, they show the sparkle of their attire with exaggerated lifting and swaying of their arms and with turns and twists.

The moon is seated on the other side of the stage. When she rises from her chair, her arm and head movements are lyrical and flowing. The stars greet her and begin to dance alone and in small circular groups. The winds pretend to be playing various instruments, such as fiddles, horns, and harps, swaying their bodies to the imaginary rhythm.

The north wind can play his part in either a mischievous or angry fashion. He upsets the circle groups by butting in and separating the clasped hands. The stars demonstrate their anger by pushing at him with thrusting arms (no actual touching). The north wind can take the baby stars for a ride in the following manner: The baby stars hold hands; the north wind breaks the hold of the ones in the middle, takes their hands, and runs, pulling them all behind him. This ride takes place in a running circle around the stage but leaving room in the front for the older stars to watch before they run up to the Queen Moon to complain.

The shooting star runs to the front and looks off in the distance (to the side from which the sun will enter); then using the same zigzag, twisting runs, he returns to the middle of the stage to swirl around the starts to notify them that the sun is coming. The stars run up to the direction from which he has come to look off in that same direction. Then together they cross to the other side to wave their goodnight to the moon. The winds with leaps and swiftly moving arms finally taper down, falling slowly to their knees or offstage, as you decide. The stars go back to the side where they originally began. With busy arms and lifted head motions, they chatter among themselves and help each other off with gowns getting ready for bed. Finally they stretch and curl up again for sleep.

The sun flows slowly on stage after the stars go to sleep. The moon and sun dance briefly together, then the moon slowly exits the way she entered, leaving her chair on stage. The play ends with the sun dancing alone in the middle of the stage using high movements to indicate brightness and light.

The Robin Family (ages 3–7)

Characters:

Daddy Robin (Handsome Robin)
Mommy Robin (Lady Robin)
Baby Robins
Sun
Cold Winds
Soft Breezes
Green growing things
Snow
Rain

The Robin Family

Once upon a time, there was a Handsome Robin. Early mornings in the spring he flew about the countryside, stopping to sing a greeting to other birds and swooping to the grasses to gather his morning breakfast.

One day, a lovely Lady Robin descended on the grass near where the robin was poking with his beak. They poked the ground together side by side for several minutes and then decided to play together. One chased the other taking turns. The Handsome Robin began to fall in love with her. And she with him. Before long, they decided to stay together and build a family. Together they built a sturdy nest high up in the cradle of a gutter safe from harsh weather and dangerous crows. They gathered twigs and dry grass, flying one by one to the nest, back and forth, packing everything down with their bodies. Finally, the nest was finished. The Lady Robin settled down to rest on the nest until the babies were hatched.

It wasn't long before a family of three Baby Robins appeared in the nest. The first thing the Baby Birds did was open their mouths and cry for food. The Daddy and Mommy Robins found worms and seeds and fed them to their babies. How hungry they were. The mommy and daddy birds barely had a rest between their flights to feed the babies.

Finally, they decided it was time the baby birds learned to fly. The Baby Birds tried, scrambling to their feet and flapping their small wings, but whoops! They fell down. The Mommy and Daddy Birds urged them to try again. The Babies tried another time, but whoops! Again they fell. Then, finally, they lifted themselves high, took courage, and flew from the nest. Soon they were swooping, flying, and trying all manner of daring tricks. After that, it was impossible to ever get them back in the nest. Flying was fun.

Soon, however, the Cold Winds began to blow. The Birds huddled in the treetops. Then the snow came, covering their nest, and the Birds became colder still. At last, Daddy and Mommy Robin said that they must fly away to the south where it was warm. The family of robins joined a formation of other birds, and all the birds together made a formation, and away they flew, far away, to the south.

The winter passed, and finally the spring returned. The Sun came out to stay. It shone on everything. Beautiful Green Things began to grow. Grass, leaves, bushes, and Plants grew everywhere. The Rain came out to help them grow, and the Soft Breezes made everything sway in the rhythm of springtime.

Then behind a flock of other birds coming over the hill, the Daddy Robin, Mommy Robin, and the whole Robin Family came flying back. They found the same tree that they had left months before and together worked to make their nest more sturdy. The Sun, the Rain, the Breezes, and the Growing Things seemed to call to them.

"Welcome back, robins, welcome home again."

Suggestions

The children are encouraged to create flying movements other than running in a circle and flapping arms up and down. The idea of exploring the corners of the room sometimes gives children the impetus to make more interesting spatial patterns. Swooping low and pretending to land from time to time can help to get them away from a routine of flapping.

The imaginary nest is on one side of the room and the birds use the whole stage to gather twigs for it. The baby robins are in the nest from the beginning, crouched over; they are not effectively seen until they are born and begin to move. The baby birds show how they cry for food by reaching and stretching on their knees, their heads turning high in every direction and their bodies twisting with great agitation. The parent robins carry the burden of balancing the stage by repeatedly moving far away from the nest to gather food and returning to feed it to the birds.

The children usually enjoy flying and flopping to show the baby birds learning to fly. Exaggerate and prolong the losing of balance because it is more fun.

The cold winds use broad arm movements, turns and runs to "blow," and the snow is indicated by shimmering movements from high to low. The birds shiver and tremble (whole-body movements). When the birds fly away, they leave the stage. Green growing things have been crouching low in a corner from the beginning. They rise slowly when the story refers to them. The sun, rain, breezes, and the green growing things move in their separate ways together. The narrator pauses to allow time for this. The robins enter in the same formation as they left. The play ends with everyone moving onstage according to the nature of their activity.

The Visits (ages 6–11)

Characters:

Pauline
Butterfly
Clouds
Sun
Stars
Moon
Worm
Roots
Insects
Goldfish
Other fish

Optional Characters:

Birds
Airplane
Underground plants
Rocks
Underwater plants
Underwater animals
Seaweed

The Visits

Pauline sat on the lawn in front of her house. She closed her book, titled *Nature's Treasures,* and looked up at the sky. How would the sky appear, she wondered, if she were able to see it not so far away but at close range? Her eyes wandered to the earth at her feet. Peering closely she thought about the things that lived underground. Then she gazed beyond the lawn, far away, and thought about the sea and the life that existed underwater. She closed her eyes and thought very hard about the wonders of nature all around her. Soon she fell asleep. And while Pauline slept, she had a dream.

***

A beautiful Butterfly appeared, landing on the book beside her. "Come with me," said the butterfly, fluttering splendid wings that were spotted with gold and crimson.

"But I can't fly," said Pauline, "How can I follow you?"

"Just think about a butterfly! Think very hard," the lovely creature said. Pauline thought very hard, and suddenly, she found herself in the air behind the Butterfly. Birds flew all around them. Higher and higher they flew. "How soft and white the clouds are," Pauline said. The Clouds sailed gently by them like fleets of sailboats on courses chartered by the wind. Sometimes they separated, drifting apart, and sometimes they gathered close together.

An Airplane went swiftly by them. Still higher they climbed until the Clouds looked like an ocean far below them. The Sun was bright, so bright that Pauline could not look at it. Then the Sun disappeared, and the Clouds below them disappeared, and the sky began to grow dark. Suddenly, Pauline saw the Stars. So splendidly they glistened all around her. Then she saw the Moon, shining clearly and brightly.

"Time to go home," the Butterfly said, and down, down, down, down they flew. At last they were on the lawn again in front of Pauline's house. She thanked the butterfly and waved goodbye to her new friend. "Come here tomorrow and look for the little worm," called the Butterfly before it disappeared behind a house.

The next day, just as the butterfly had said, a little Worm wiggled its way near to where Pauline sat. The book was open beside her, and the Worm crawled busily over the page as if he were investigating every word. Pauline realized he was studying and did not interrupt him. Finally, he looked up and saw her, and in a most cordial manner, he asked, "Would you care to see what I see under the ground?"

"Oh, yes!" Pauline replied excitedly. "But how can I get there?" "Just think about a worm. Think very hard and then follow me." She did as the worm suggested, and a moment later she found herself below the earth. Roots of all kinds twisted and curved and stretched out around her. Roots of trees grew long and strong in many different directions. Insects of odd shapes and sizes crawled about them, each appearing to have a special job to do. Worms like her polite and friendly guide were wriggling here and there in every direction. There were Rocks of different forms and colors. And Pauline saw a wonderland of vegetables and vines. At last, the Worm told her that they must make their way to the surface. When they came out of the darkness into the light, Pauline was surprised to find herself by the edge of the sea.

"Wait here," said the Worm, bowing low to her from his many waists. "A Goldfish will presently arrive to take you on another trip. Good day, my dear."

"Oh, thank you, thank you for the visit underground," Pauline called after him, but he had already wormed his way out of sight.

A moment later, just as the worm predicted, a bright and lively Goldfish popped his head out of the water.

"Are you going to take me for a visit under the sea?" Pauline asked gaily before the goldfish had a chance to speak.

"Of course," answered the Fish, jumping and spinning in the air, diving in and out of the water and showing off outrageously for her.

"But first you must think of a goldfish—a clever, talented, gorgeous goldfish!"

That was easy. Pauline could think of nothing else with the Goldfish splashing around her like that. And the next thing she knew, she was under the sea. At her feet were the most beautiful shells she had ever seen. Fish that she had read about, fish that she had heard about, and fish that she had never read or heard or imagined about swam all around her. Plants and Flowers of brilliant colors covered the ocean floor and twisted about in the water making intricate patterns of line and color. She saw starfish, clams, crabs, lobsters, shrimp, crawfish, turtles, and many strange animals of the sea. Led by the Goldfish, who seemed to know every living thing they passed, Pauline wandered for hours among Rocks rubbed smooth by the water and looked in wonderment at the treasures of the sea as they floated by her.

At last the Goldfish turned and said, "It's time we head for home." Pauline was sad to leave, but she followed the Goldfish to the surface and found herself by the shore again.

The Goldfish flipped himself in the air a few times and said, "Some form, eh? But I can't see you home. I am sorry about that, but my tricks don't work on land. You wouldn't believe what a flop they are out there!"

"Oh, that's quite all right. I'll find my way," Pauline replied. "Thank you for taking me under the sea. It was truly exciting!"

The goldfish did a double flip in the air and almost banged his head on a rock.

***

Pauline opened her eyes. She stretched and gazed up at the treetops. Then she looked thoughtfully at the book lying beside her. All at once a colorful Butterfly flew past her. Swiftly, Pauline jumped to her feet and began to chase it, wondering with strange anticipation where the beautiful creature might lead her.

Suggestions

Because there are so many characters and episodes in this story it would be both confusing and limiting to suggest movement. The characters may be interpreted the way children see them, but prior discussion is necessary to effectively visualize the scenes.

This story is especially suitable for a large class since it provides everyone with parts without being crowded for space at any one time. The story should be altered to include exhibits and specimens of nature that may be in the classroom or that might be suggested by the children. Reading the story once through, discussing it, and choosing parts are all that are necessary to launch this on its way. Push the furniture far back against the wall. Note that the story can be simplified as much as you wish, your children merely exploring the moving things underground and becoming alert to what they see all around them. Bringing in pictures of the living things mentioned and asking the children to do the same enriches the project.

A Magic Sewing Box (ages 5–11)
Characters:

Tailor
Tailor's wife
Sewing needle
Scissors
Straight pins
Spools of colored thread

Optional Characters:

Children (optional number, change in story to fit)
Tailor's assistant

A Magic Sewing Box

Once upon a time there lived a Tailor, his Wife and their seven lovely Children. The man was a fine tailor and made clothes that were fit for a king to wear. But although many people came to his shop to buy his garments, he could not sew fast enough to provide enough food for his large family. The tailor's Wife tried to help him, but she was very busy tending the children and had little time to spare.

One evening, the Tailor watched sadly as his Wife put the children to sleep. Then he said to her, "We do not have enough money to buy food for the children. We must send them away to be cared for until we are able to provide for them." The tailor's Wife began to weep. The good man comforted her as best he could. "I am sorry," he said, "but they are hungry, and there is nothing else we can do."

That night, while the tailor and his family were sleeping, a strange and wonderful thing happened. The Sewing Needle jumped out of the pin cushion and pointed to all the colorful Spools of thread asleep in the sewing box.

"Wake up, lazy spools!" he called. "Did you hear the poor tailor talking to his wife today?" Without waiting for an answer, he continued calling to them, hastening around the room awakening them. "We must help him. Wake up! Wake up!"

The Spools roused themselves, stood tall, and bent their wide ears to the needle.

"Tonight," he said, "while the tailor and his good wife are sleeping, WE shall make the clothes for him. You there, Mr. Cutting Shears. Get busy! Cut the patterns from this cloth. Stand UP, Straight Pins! Connect the pieces of material and hold them fast while I lead the thread around. Come! Come! We have no time to lose!"

Swiftly across the cloth, the Scissors leaped. Here, there, and everywhere the Straight Pins jumped. In and out, weaved the colorful threads as the sturdy Needle showed the way. All night long, the Needle, Thread, Pins, and Scissors worked: cutting, pulling sections together, sewing them fast. At last they finished. When dawn came through the windows, the exhausted sewing-box workers climbed back into their places in the box.

Well, when the Tailor awoke, you can image his surprise! Handsome suits and dresses lay all about the floor. He raced to his Wife and awakened her. Together they danced for joy around the room! Then gathering all the clothes in their arms they set out for the marketplace to sell them.

The next day, all the clothes were sold, and with the money, they bought food for the children and themselves. Enough money was left over to hire an Assistant to help the tailor.

From that day on, the Tailor, his Wife, and his Children had a good life with plenty of food for all of them. But never did they discover the strange and wonderful magic of the sewing box.

Suggestions

The tailor and his wife move sadly as they work. With exaggerated motions, he sews and she does broad spatial movements such as sweeping the floor. If children are included in the cast, they can enter and begin playing imaginary games. Some can stand (jumping rope or playing ball), and some kneel, pretending to play cards or chess. The wife puts them to bed either by waving them to follow her offstage or settling them down toward the rear of the stage, where they yawn and stretch and lie down. She returns to do the sad pantomime with the tailor, after which they both go to sleep in a corner. The sewing-box contents have been crouching in the middle of the room from the beginning.

The sewing needle moves all over the floor during his speech. After the sewing supplies have done their work, they go back to their original places. When the tailor and his wife go to the marketplace, they circle the whole stage, and the second time around, the children join them. Everyone comes joyfully as if into the room. An assistant enters, and they greet him warmly. As the story ends, the mother plays with the children toward the rear of the stage, and the tailor and his assistant sew cheerfully in the center. All the contents in the sewing box then join in.

The Treasure Chest (ages 6–11)
Characters:

Swimmers
Jewels
Fabrics
Coins
Musical Instruments

Optional Characters:

Anything the children might hope to find in a treasure chest under the sea

The Treasure Chest

It was a summer afternoon, and Bob and Mike had gone exploring underwater in their snorkels, masks, and fins. They were collecting shells, searching all along the ocean floor for specimens. Suddenly, they came upon a strange-looking object. It was a chest, almost completely covered with thick strands of seaweed. Bob and Mike tore the seaweed away and peered to see a way to open it. The chest must have been there for years and years. They found the handles of the lid and together pulled and pulled to try to lift it open. With all their weight, they pressed against the chest and pushed some more, and slowly, very slowly, the heavy lid of the chest began to lift. They pushed some more, as hard as they could, just a little more, and did it. Finally, the cover fell back, and they were able to peer inside. The strange box was filled to the brim with treasures.

Bob reached inside and pulled out Jewelry made with precious stones—rubies, emeralds, diamonds, and pearls. The Jewels sparkled around him. Then Mike put his hand in and brought out heavy Cloths of exotic textures—velvet, brocade, and satin. Bob looked again and found boxfuls of Coins from different lands. As he gathered them, the Coins clattered and jingled. Then the boys found Musical Instruments—horns, harmonicas, fiddles, and mandolins. Amazingly, the instruments began to play themselves. What a cacophony of sound!

But the boys needed to swim soon to the surface, they had been below for a long time. Quickly, Bob and Mike piled the treasures back into the chest and closed the cover. They swam to the surface. There they looked all about the landscape to find a landmark. But in every direction there was nothing to see but water. How would we ever find this place again? One said to the other. We won't, said the other. Sadly, they knew that they would never be able to find the chest again when they returned with help, and the chest was too heavy to move. Sorrowfully, they swam back to their boat. The treasure chest would no doubt stay forever, undisturbed, at the bottom of the sea. But Bob and Mile wondered for many years thereafter how the treasure came to rest right there where they alone discovered it. Could it all have been a dream? So real.

Suggestions

Spending some time describing as a group what these treasures look like, sound like, and feel like will open the children to the sense of being there. Actually visualizing the scene—the water the boys are swimming in, the treasure chest they discover, and the multiple kinds of treasures inside—constitutes both the fun and learning in the adventure. The discussion period should involve ideas about other treasures. At that time, practice improvisations on some of the actions that will appear in the story, such as trying to open a heavy lid under pressure; swimming with high, low, and wide strokes through heavy waves; interpreting sparkling jewels with body movements; and showing heavy fabrics of different textures and jingling coins, and whatever other treasures are to be found.

All swimming movements are done standing. Looking for shells should be done from corner to corner of the room to encourage broad spatial patterns. Swimmers should find the imaginary treasure chest toward the rear center of the stage so that the treasures will have room to move in front of it. How to interpret the possibility that it is all a dream leave up to the children, perhaps inquiring if any of *their* dreams have seemed real.

The Shoe Tree (ages 5–10)
Characters:

Farmer
Farmer's Wife
Many Children
Old Woman

The Shoe Tree

A Farmer lived with his Wife and their many Children in a little cottage by the edge of the forest. The Farmer earned his livelihood by growing and selling vegetables that he cultivated in a field behind his house. He worked hard to provide his family with food and shelter, but he could afford to buy them little else. It saddened him that his children had no presentable shoes to wear to school, although they never complained. All summer long, when the Children were not in school, they helped the farmer care for the land. Shortly before school was about to reopen, the harvest of vegetables was ready and the children were dispatched to the marketplace. The Children set out through the woods toward the town. But after walking for several hours, they realized that they had lost their way. They wandered on, not knowing which way to turn. At last, since they were very tired, they stopped to rest against a tree.

In the distance, a small, white-haired Old Woman approached them from the other direction. When she drew nearer, the children observed that she was dressed in a worn and limp-hanging coat, but on her feet were the most magnificent shoes they had ever laid eyes on. As they stared, the Old Woman paused and looked back at the curious group. She saw their ragged shoes and surmised what they were thinking. She looked up at their faces and smiled.

"You like the shoes I'm wearing, I betcha," she said in a cheerful trilling voice that sounded like a song.

"They're beautiful," one of the Children replied, while the others quickly nodded in agreement.

"They are the shoes of a fine dancer," the woman explained, "and made especially for her."

"Really? But who is the dancer?"

"Why, she is me," the woman responded.

"I don't understand." The Children shook their heads, waiting for her to continue.

"You see, I worked hard for the shoes. I studied and trained and practiced every day. They fit me perfectly, don't you agree?"

"Oh yes," The Children agreed, for they had seen her walk fast and gracefully across the forest, in spite of her age.

The Old Woman gazed up at the tree's highest branches their tips appearing to touch the sky. She thought for a moment and smiled. "If this tree standing here was not an oak but a shoe tree, holding not acorns in its branches but shoes—oh, many different kinds of shoes—which would you choose?" The Children walked slowly around the tree, looking high up at its branches; then they sat down beneath it thinking.

Finally, one Child jumped to her feet. "I would choose dancer's shoes like you have," she exclaimed.

"And what would you do if they were yours and they fit you to a tee?" the Woman asked.

"Why, I would dance!" And so saying, she began to dance about the clearing. When she had finished her dance and joined the others under the tree, the Woman pointed to another Child. "And you?" she inquired.

"Me? I would take fireman's boots," he replied, "thick and heavy ones."

"And what would you do with them?" she asked.

The Child rose to his feet bending under the weight of an imaginary hose. Striding through the forest floor, he shouted "Fire! Fighting fire! Crushing burning wood to ash!"

The old woman asked each Child in turn to choose the shoes they would feel most excited to own. One chose a track runner's shoes. Another, the soft white shoes of a nurse taking care of the sick. One Child selected lumberjack's boots for cutting down trees. Another child tried to latch onto skies. And the last to choose took figure skates.

For the rest of the afternoon, the Children skated, skied, worked, ran, put out fires, cut lumber, and danced, pretending to be the people of the shoes, and the Old Woman watched them all. Then she shared with them her hamper of food.

While they were eating, the Woman explained that even though they were only pretending now, whatever they truly wanted the shoes to be, might become real. "For if you set your sights on the shoes as you did on the highest branches of this tree and then work hard to reach them, they will be yours."

The Woman gathered her things and then gave the oldest Child directions to the marketplace but not the one they had set out for. "This marketplace is four miles farther and across a stream, but your vegetables are more needed there because few farmers live in the town, and you will get a better price. Can you make the trip?"

The Children felt so full of energy that they agreed without hesitation and set off. They waved goodbye to the Woman as she continued cheerfully on her way. With difficulty, the Children walked the extra miles. They waded across the stream by stepping very slowly and balancing carefully on the slippery stones. Finally, they saw the unfamiliar town in the distance and ran the final quarter mile to the market-place. What the woman said was true, for the harvest sold for almost twice the value they had expected.

When the Children arrived home at last, their Parents greeted them joyfully. With the extra money they had received at the marketplace, each child was able to have new shoes with which to start the school year.

In the months and years to follow, the Children did not talk together very much about the old woman and the "shoe tree," but they never forgot the meaning of her words as they gazed high up at the treetops on their way to school. And some of the Children came to wear shoes they might never have dared to try on. And they wore them very well indeed!

Suggestions

In the beginning, the farmer and his family are tending the field with exaggerated movements of planting, shoveling, raking, and picking. The work should be animated and busy.

The farmer and his wife can pretend to tie kerchiefs around the girls' heads and pat the boys on the back as they load them up with vegetables and send them off to the marketplace.

Show wandering through the forest by children casting their heads high in many directions as they trudge a wide path around the existing space. The feeling of being lost is conveyed by progressively accelerating the tempo of movement and increasing sudden changes of direction. When the old woman appears, the children should move toward her and back, near her and away, as they regard her cautiously from head to toe. When the old woman "speaks," she should move in broad spatial patterns to show her command of things. When the children speak, they should do the same, by turning, stretching, bending, leaping, and other "big" movements. In other words, the ones speaking should stand out from the others onstage. Little motions of the face and hands do not come across.

In the preparation *prior* to enacting the story, the children decide what shoes they will select in the forest. The leader can call on them by name during the story, allowing sufficient time between each for interpretation. Any kind of shoes can be used: shoes of professional people, tradesmen, even storybook characters. Ideas need not be limited to actual shoes such as sneakers or boots. Selection is intended to imply the purpose and activity of the shoe wearer, not actual footwear.

The meal is shared using arm and head pantomime while sitting in a ragged circle. The old woman rises and moves about the room as she talks, with high movements toward the branches and low movements toward the seated children.

They bid one another goodbye with broad arm patterns. The old woman dances off, like the dancer she is, and the children set off for the new market with spirited turns and skips, moving in several wide circular paths around the room to show distance.

When they wade across the stream, they balance on stepping-stones with arms outstretched, wavering to show the slippery stones. One or two can lose their balance and fall, then be helped up by others. When they see the unfamiliar new town in the distance, they stop and peer out at it (toward where they will soon exit) and then show their excitement (perhaps by holding hands and skipping in a circle). They leave the "stage" as the reader describes their good fortune in the marketplace.

The mother and father come on stage, working the field as in the beginning. The children come back onstage (arriving home), and a broad welcome ensues, parents and children pretending to hug and then dancing happily about. The play ends as the children become deep in thought and look up high, pointing as if at giant treetops. The words of the reader will carry this ending, followed by applause signaling the end.

Robert the Rabbit (ages 3–6)

Characters:

Fish
Leaves
Rabbits
Robert the Rabbit
Tooth Fairy

Optional Characters:

Deer
Squirrels
Birds
Chipmunks

Robert the Rabbit

Robert was a rabbit who was very good at hopping. He liked hopping. He hopped all over the fields to find carrots to eat, and he hopped all through the woods to find Rabbit friends to play with. But what Robert really wanted to do was dance. Oh, if he could only dance, he thought, how happy he would be!

Every day, Robert looked at the Leaves dancing in the wind, twirling along the ground and leaping in the air. If only he could dance like that, he thought. He gazed into the pond and saw the Fish dancing in the water, skirting high and low, swirling this way and that through the waves. If only he too could dance that way! But he could only hop—up and down high and low, fast and slow, hop, hop, hop.

One day, when Robert was playing hide-and-seek with his Friends, he realized that one of his teeth was loose. This made him very happy, because he knew that when the tooth fell out, he would receive a visit from the Tooth Fairy. Like the other rabbits, he would put the tooth deep inside his burrow at night under his pillow and dream of the wish he wanted the Tooth Fairy to grant. In the morning, he would know if the Fairy had come and taken his tooth, giving him his wish in return. Of course, Robert knew what he would wish for. He wanted to dance!

The tooth became looser and looser. Robert had to give all his carrots to the other Rabbits because he could not chew them. At last, one evening after supper, the tooth fell out. Robert went to sleep with the tooth tucked safely under his pillow.

That night he dreamed that the beautiful Tooth Fairy appeared. All the Animals of the fields and woodlands came out to dance with her—the Deer, the Squirrels, the Chipmunks, even the Birds. It was a lovely dream.

When morning came, Robert woke up. He looked under his pillow. The tooth was gone! Robert jumped out of his bed and raced from the burrow. He did not stop until he came to the field where the Leaves were dancing in the air and the Fish were dancing in the pond. He began to dance too. He danced all over the field and the woodlands and the carrot patch. To some of his Rabbit friends, it seemed as though he was still hopping, but that is because they did not know what dancing was. Robert had always known.

Suggestions

Robert is on stage throughout except during his dream. In reading, pause after he first finds "friends to play with" so all the rabbits have a chance to hop about with one another, playing games. The friends leave the stage soon after coming on, and Robert is left alone, thinking. He sways and moves sadly with slow, round movements of his arms and downcast tosses of his head.

The leaves and the fish stay low on separate sides of the stage toward the rear and remain on stage throughout, rising to dance at specified times during the story.

The rabbit friends play hide and seek (choosing places to crouch as if hiding, then jumping out to be found), while Robert thinks about his loose tooth. He sighs with his whole body as he gives away his carrots. The rabbits thank him with sympathetic and understanding movements and exit.

Robert curls up in a corner to sleep. The Tooth Fairy enters and dances alone. Then, if the size of the class permits, animals of the woodland arrive and dance with her, one group (or person) at a time.

Robert comes out of the burrow and dances with the leaves and fish. They continue dancing until the end. At the close of the story, Robert is joined by all the other rabbits and animals of the fields and woodland. They hop and leap and jump around Robert as the story ends.

A Smile in the Snow (ages 4–10)

Characters:

Wind
Snow
Meg
Timothy
Carol
Snowman
Snow Fairy

Optional Characters:

Night
Icicles
Snow-covered branches
Moon
Sun

A Smile in the Snow

It was winter. The Wind was blowing hard and made the air quite cold and Snow began to fall. The Snow fell all day, on the earth, on the trees, and on the houses, until all the ground was deeply covered. When the Snow stopped falling, Meg, Timothy, and Carol came out to play.

"Let's build a snowman," Timothy said.

"A good idea!" the other children called out, and they began to gather snow. Bigger and bigger the Snowman became as more and more snow was gathered from all over the yard and piled upon him.

At last the Snowman was built. Meg placed two stones in his face for eyes. Carol put a stick in for a nose and was just about to make his mouth when Timothy splashed her from behind with snow.

"C'mon, snow fight!" he called.

'I'm going to get you, Timothy, just wait," Meg said. "Come on, Carol, let's get him."

They threw snowballs all afternoon, sending streams of snow into the air, then building a snow fort, laughing, and screaming. Until slowly, Night stole upon them, making the lawn darker and darker.

"It's getting dark," Carol said. "We'd better go inside."

"We have to finish the snowman first," said Meg. She picked up a handful of snow and pressed it into the snowman's face to form a wide smile. It fell down.

"Here, let me try," said Timothy. From a tree, he took a curving twig that looked to him exactly like a smile. He wedged it into the snowman's face. But it, too, fell down.

Carol was gathering stones. "These will surely stay," she announced. She placed each one carefully on the snowman's face, and for a moment, he seemed to smile. But the last stones on each side fell off, and the snowman looked very grim indeed. So did the children. They tried everything, but nothing seemed to work! The snowman looked silly without a smile. At last they could no longer see as darkness spread over the yard. The Children scampered into their house to go to sleep.

***

While the children were asleep, the Snow Fairy appeared. She danced over the frozen ground, taking in the beauty that was all around her. Icicles bedecked the night like jewelry, and slender Snow-Covered Branches glistened and seemed to wave to her. Then the Snow Fairy came upon the Snowman. She wondered why he looked so sad. She touched him with her magic wand. He looked at her and shook himself so that powdery snow drifted into the air.

"Why are you sad, little man?" the Fairy asked.

The Snowman replied, "I want to play in the snow, just like the children played. I watched them, and I am sad because I cannot leave the spot where I was made."

"Oh dear, I do understand," said the Fairy. Then busily, she searched through the glistening sandbag she carried over her shoulder. She pulled at this and that and at last was satisfied. Rubbing a cloth against her cheek, she then touched the snowman's cheek.

"Now my friend, for as long as the night remains, you can play and have fun in the snow." She stepped back and watched with delight as he jumped out into the snow.

How happy the Snowman felt! He slid and rolled in the snow, he skated on the ice, he made snow statues, he tossed mounds of snow in the air. He played all night long. Then, too soon, the Sun began to creep into the sky.

"Back you go, little man," said the Fairy, and she touched him once again. Then she disappeared. The night too was disappearing slowly and silently as the Sun approached.

The bright Sun awakened the Children. They rubbed the sleep from their eyes and dressed quickly. Then they went outside. There was the Snowman, just as they had left him. Meg and Carol and Timothy ran toward him. Could it be the same snowman? How different he appeared. The children studied him in amazement for there on his face, from cheek to cheek for all to see, was a grand and glorious smile in the snow.

Suggestions

Allow the wind time to move before the snow starts. The wind continually changes directions and is sometimes fast, sometimes slow. Snowflakes should have cascading turns and movements from high to low, showing with head, arms, and hands the sparkle of snow. Children build the snowman by going out to the far corners of the stage to gather snow and returning each time to pile it on the snowman.

A black cape, scarf, or piece of material would be effective and provide interesting material for a child to work with to interpret night.

When the smiles will not stay on the snowman, the children express their dismay by broad arm movements of exasperation. Then when night moves about in the middle of the stage, the children go off to a corner and slowly, with stretching and sleepy movements, curl up to sleep, The moon enters and dances. The Snow Fairy dances and is joined by the icicles and the snow-covered branches.

All the night characters move quietly in the background when the snowman begins to play in the snow. The snowman must make his movements bigger than real play, creating an improvisation of throwing snow and dodging snow balls.

After the Fairy taps the snowman, he goes back to his place, and all the night figures move slowly off the stage, still in character, opposite where the sun is entering. The sun dances all over the stage, awakening the children by spreading rays of sunlight. The children rise and approach the snowman. When they notice his smile, they show their surprise by turns and skips, moving cheerfully around him.

The House on the Hill (ages 5–10)

Characters:

Paul
Jan
Old man
Dutch dolls

French dolls
Israeli dolls
Japanese dolls
Norwegian dolls
Spanish dolls
Russian dolls

The House on the Hill

One day, Paul and Jan were playing on a hillside. They picked
flowers and then played hide-and-seek among the trees that
lined the slope. When it began to get dark the children realized that they had wandered quite far from the path. They
looked all about to find a pathway that would lead them
home again. Then suddenly, they came upon a house.

Paul and Jan ventured closer to the house, trying to peer
through its windows, which were tightly shut with dark cur-
tains covering them from the inside. Curious about finding
a lone house hidden here among the trees, they pushed the
door. It was unlocked. Frightened, Paul wanted to go away
from the house at once. But Jan was bold and adventurous.
"Let's explore," she said with confidence. "And besides,
maybe someone's here who can show us the way home." At
that Paul agreed, and cautiously they stepped inside.

As soon as the children closed the door behind them, they
saw an unusual sight. Out of another doorway marched a
row of Dolls each as big as they themselves were, and each
dressed in clothes of different countries. Immediately, the
Children were fascinated. They raced around the Dolls,
touching their costumes and their shoes and their colorful
hats.

They were so busy, they did not notice a door opening
behind them. Turning suddenly, they saw a frowning Man
with a long white beard and a white robe tied with a silver
cord. He was very angry! He yelled at the children, waving
a cane wildly and stamping his feet. "What's the meaning of
this!" he roared, so thunderously the poor Children huddled together in fright.

"What are you doing in my house? What are you doing with my dolls?"

"Please sir, nothing," Jan answered in a trembling voice. She gestured with her arms toward the door by which they had entered and said, "We lost our way and came upon your house by accident. We thought perhaps you might show us the way to the town. When we came in, we saw these dolls, and honestly, sir, we would not do them any harm. They are beautiful!"

"So, you like my doll collection, eh?" the odd Man bellowed. Then he smiled and quite astounded the children who were now shaking with fear by asking, "Would you like to see them dance?"

"Oh, yes," the Children screamed together.

The Man, suddenly jolly now and laughing merrily, went to a corner of the room and pressed a large silver button. The Children were amazed to see the Dutch Dolls with their wooden shoes begin to dance around the room just as if they were live children like themselves. When they had finished, they went directly back to their places in the line and looked as though they had never moved at all.

The Man clapped his hands with delight. "Do you want to see some more?"

"Oh, yes," the Children answered. "Can you make the others dance?"

The Man pushed another silver button, and this time the little French Dolls began to dance, kicking up their heels and tipping their black berets. When the dance was over, the Dolls went back to the line just as the dolls before them had done. Each of the Dolls danced when the old man pressed a special silver button. The old man watched with pride and sometimes even danced along with them.

The Scotch Dolls, dressed in kilts, played the bagpipes as they did their lively Scottish folk dance. The Israeli Dolls did a dance of water, telling a story of how water in the desert is carefully collected and dispersed to make plants and trees grow on their land. The Japanese Dolls danced with fast little steps in colorful long kimonos. The Norwegian Dolls, dressed for skating, danced as if they were on ice instead of in a room. The Spanish Dolls, with their fans waving and lace dresses swirling, turned and stamped their heels as they danced. The straight-backed Russian Dolls, in high black boots, crossed their arms and kicked their feet as they whirled about the room.

"Your dolls are beautiful," the Children shouted when the dances were over, "the most beautiful dolls in the world, and we shall never forget this day! Thank you!"

The man beamed with pride. "Yes," he said rubbing his hands together, "they are beautiful, and I am going to let other children come to see them as well. From now on, my house will be open, and I will push the silver buttons for all the children who wish to see my dolls."

The old man gave the children directions for finding their way home, and he waved to them as they ran down the hillside. "Come back, come back, soon," he called.

Many times afterward, the children returned to the strange house on the hill to see the marvelous dancing dolls. And so did other children from all over the land, from that very day to this.

Suggestions

While interpreting the first paragraph, the children should use all the space around them. Flower picking and playing hide-and-seek are used to encourage high and low movements in many directions. Looking about for the pathway home should make them run and lean searchingly from corner to corner, peering out into the distance. Their surprise at seeing the house should be registered with some sudden movement of the torso, head, and arms.

Fear and boldness should be expressed in movement and pantomime as the children move cautiously around the imaginary house.

As soon as they enter, the dolls march out stiffly, one behind the other, and form a row across the room. The children investigate them, touching their costumes and moving behind the row in wonder and amazement. The angry man must exaggerate every step to show his agitation. He can be made to look silly or angry, laughable or frightening, according to individual interpretation.

While the bolder child speaks, the man continues to jump around, looking at his dolls and making sure they are all right.

Other movements are explained in the story as they occur. The costumes are only indications of what the children should be showing off as they dance. Show a full skirt with wide turns and circular arm movements. Long kimonos might be indicated by fast tiny steps and adding staccato arm and finger movements to show the silk designs. After each dance, the children should imitate the dolls before the old man pushes the next button.

The old man continues to move in his jumpy, excitable way as he talks to the children about coming back and as he shows them the way home. The play ends as he waves to them, and they wave back, disappearing off stage. Naturally, the play can be done with fewer dolls, depending on the size and attention span of the group.

The History Class (ages 7–11)

Characters:

Teacher
Students (any number)

The History Class

Mr. Peterson called the class to order. "Good morning, students," he said. "I hope you have all completed your homework. When I call your names, I want you to report on the lesson that we studied yesterday in class about the Civil War. Now then, let's begin. Michael, what was one of the principal causes of the Civil War?"

Michael stood and came to the front of the class. He told about the slaves and how they had to plant the cotton and tobacco and harvest the fields under the hot plantation sun.

He told how sad and difficult their lives were. Then he told about Lincoln, calling the nation "a house divided—half slave and half free" and proclaiming that *all* people should be free. Dave and Tommy raised their hands, and when Mr. Peterson called on them, they described the way the war was fought, the Union North fighting against the Confederate South with rifles and cannons, on horseback and on foot.

Then Bruce and Tina raised their hands and told the class about the ending of the war. They described the way Robert E. Lee, the brave and beloved general of the South, surrendered in a courthouse in Virginia to the determined general of the North, Ulysses S. Grant. Then the slaves were freed, and the people of the North celebrated victory.

Mr. Peterson called on Jennifer and Amy who told how Lincoln was assassinated, shot by John Wilkes Booth at Ford's Theatre in Washington, five days after Lee's surrender.

Mr. Peterson praised the students for their descriptions and urged them to read more about this tragedy in American history, ending the class saying that the country slowly came together as one nation, reconciling its differences.

Suggestions

This format can be used to interpret any other facet of history that has suitable action.

The teacher uses about a third of the room for his pantomime. The students sit facing him in chairs or on the floor on the opposite side of the room. This leaves maximum space for movements between the teacher's chair and the students' chairs. If the teacher is made to be rather stern, it will be more fun for the group and also easier to pantomime. Students are called by their real names. During the preparation preceding the play, the children can discuss the Civil War and can decide what aspect of it they want to show. Interpretations by the children of horseback riding, cannon firing, shooting, and fighting are important in order for them to feel comfortable in interpreting history in this manner. The slaves—their work, their hardships while being captive—should be discussed and interpreted. Their eventual emancipation and the continued need for equality in race relations are not impossible to talk about as well.

Students, for example, Dave and Tommy in one situation, can take separate sides of the subject they are interpreting—Dave, the Union Army, against Tommy, the Confederate. When Jennifer and Amy are called, one can play Lincoln being shot and the other, John Wilkes Booth. Students return to their chairs after each improvisation.

The key to the success of this story, and to others that a leader can compose according to subjects being studied, is an informal communication of ideas. It should be noted that the first time this is done with a class it will probably be a little strange. Ask for suggestions from the students about a class lesson they might like to bring to life.

The Speed and Fury of Fire (ages 5–11)

Characters:

Campers, boys, and girls
Fire
Wind
Rain

The Speed and Fury of Fire

A group of Campers were walking in the woods when they came upon a clearing. They began to look for dry wood to make a fire, for it was growing cold. Some found a dead tree standing on the edge of the clearing and chopped it down with their hatchets. Others collected timber and snapped dry branches into pieces with their feet. They brought all the wood to the clearing and made a fire. As it began to blaze the Campers stood around it and became quite warm. All of a sudden, the Wind began to blow harshly. It blew against the birch trees and made them sway, it blew against the Campers and made them duck and run for cover, but worst of all, it blew around the Fire and made it grow and spread away from its small enclosure of rocks. The children were worried and tried to think of a way to stop the fire. They emptied all the water in their canteens on the blaze, but it was not enough.

The Wind was blowing harder than before. The Campers tried desperately to smother the fire by pouring armfuls of dirt on it. This helped to quell the fire in places where it blazed but could not stop it from spreading. The Fire was edging out of the clearing; soon it would attack the surrounding woodland.

All at once the Campers looked up into the sky and saw a large black cloud. In a moment a torrent of Rain descended on the woods. The Fire was pressed to the ground as the rain beat down on it. The fire had met its match in the rain. The Campers were overjoyed, so nearly had there been a disaster. They danced in the pouring rain around the embers.

Then the Wind died away and the Rain stopped. The Campers gathered their gear and started for home, wet but wiser about the speed and fury of fire.

Suggestions

Pause reading when the campers are chopping the trees to take advantage of the action possibilities. Those who are interpreting fire huddle in the middle of the room. As the fire grows, they rise slowly to their knees moving torso, head, and arms in twisted, flame-like movements. The campers meanwhile move contentedly about the fire, rubbing their arms in warming motions.

The cold wind enters with broad, sweeping arm movements, leaping in changing directions across the room. The spreading fire might show its spreading by standing together in a group in the center of the room stretching arms and legs outward to all sides, some edging beyond the center in all directions.

The rain can begin as clouds entering, shown by several children storming in who then become the downfall of rain. The fire goes slowly back to its original place, although sporadic movements continue to show the embers. The wind

and rain slow their movements and exit. The campers collect their imaginary gear onto their backpacks and exit as if
chattering to each other and looking with wizened glances
back at the coals.

Discussion should include the characteristics of fire and
how fire both helps and threatens our lives, showing specific
examples.

A Small Statue (ages 3–9)

Characters:

Sculptor
Clay dancer

A Small Statue

A sculptor decided to create a dancer out of clay. He built
an armature of wire, kneaded and wedged his clay, and then
began to build up his figure. The sculptor worked eagerly
with his wooden and wire tools. Frequently, he stepped back
to regard his work with a critical eye. He worked for many
days on his sculpture, going to sleep exhausted and awakening fresh and eager to sculpt her in more detail. At last
the dancer was completed to his satisfaction. The sculptor
signed his name on the back of the statue and went to sleep.

While he was asleep, he had a dream. In the dream, the
little dancer began to move. Slowly at first . . . an arm . . . a
leg . . . her head . . . her body. Then more boldly, the arms
began to bend and curve.

She seemed very happy to be moving. Soon, she stepped
right out of her base, leaving two small holes where her
feet had been. She began to dance around the studio.
She danced from corner to corner as if exploring her new
space. She leaped high in the air, full of joy to be dancing.
She spun around as if to see everything at once. On and
on, the statue danced. But when dawn came and the sky
began to lighten, the dancer stepped back into her base,
placing her feet right back into the tiny holes.

The sculptor opened his eyes and stretched. He rose and went straight to his worktable to look at the new statue. There she was, as fine a piece of sculpture as he had ever made. Then all at once he remembered his dream.

"She does look real," he thought and then laughed. "What a funny thing to dream."

What a funny thing to dream, the small statue seemed to say.

Suggestions

The sculptor must make his movements very broad, moving away from the statue and returning to it as he works, remembering that he is not really modeling clay but making an improvisation of this activity. At the end of the story, when he looks at his statue again and laughs (as the dancer stands motionless), he does this with a bubbly movement of his whole body. When his back is turned, the dancer can make a small head motion to indicate her mysterious achievement.

The Baby Bud (ages 3–9)

Characters:

> Plants becoming Flowers
> Sun
> Rain
> Baby bud,
> Elizabeth
> Children
> Elizabeth's mother

The Baby Bud

It was spring and all over the garden Plants began to sprout. The plants grew taller and taller, forming full green leaves. Flower buds began to open and colorful petals appeared. That is what happened to most of the flowers. But one little flower happened to have been planted underneath the window ledge of a house. She could never grow enough to open and so she remained a tiny Bud.

Each morning, the Sun came out to shine upon the flowers, and as they drank in the warm sunlight, they grew taller and stronger. The Sun tried to shine upon the little bud, but alas, it just could not reach her where she was. The Rain came often and showered down upon the flowers. As the Flowers drank the water, their stems became sturdy and their colors more beautiful. The Rain tried hard to reach the little bud, but the window ledge of the house was in the way.

The other Flowers laughed at the little bud and called her "Baby Bud."

"What a funny thing she is," they said. "She has no colorful petals or handsome green leaves as we have," and they turned their pretty heads away from her and would not answer when she nodded to them. Indeed, the Baby Bud tried hard to get their attention, for she was quite lonely and unhappy to be where she was.

One day, a group of Children came into the garden to pick some flowers. They were delighted to find so many tall and colorful flowers, and they picked as many of these as their arms could carry. They did not even glance at the baby bud, for they wanted only the biggest and the brightest blossoms. Then laughing and all talking together, they ran off, the pretty flowers cradled in their arms.

But on the way home, they decided to play games. They dropped their flowers and played one game and then another. They played all afternoon. The lovely Flowers were left alone and forgotten, and soon they began to wilt. Fresh flowers, as everyone knows, need water to drink after they are picked from the earth.

When the Children returned, they found all their flowers dried out and almost dead, and they were very unhappy. Most of the Children went home, but one little girl named Elizabeth felt so bad about what she had done that she decided to go back into the garden and gather more flowers.

When she arrived, she looked all over the garden but saw nothing left except for the baby bud, all by itself under the window ledge of the house. She plucked it very carefully and carried it home. This time she did not stop along the way. Instead, she placed it at once in a glass of water by the window. The Sun poured through the glass and was glad to reach the bud at last. The Water in the glass was able to give the little flower all the nourishment it needed. Before long, the Baby Bud began to grow.

Larger and larger it grew. Presently, the Bud began to open. Beautiful golden petals appeared, and it became more lovely than any of the other flowers had been. Elizabeth beamed with joy and pride, and she showed the flower to her mother.

Her Mother smiled and said, "You see, Elizabeth, the other flowers were larger and prettier, but because they were unloved and uncared for, they shriveled up. Your baby bud, which was once so tiny, is beautiful now because you loved and cared for it."

Elizabeth was very happy. The Sun and the Rain seemed happy too. But the beautiful golden Baby Bud must have been the happiest of all.

Suggestions

The flowers and the baby bud are "onstage," spread apart and crouching low. They all begin to grow together, but as the other flowers rise to a standing position, the baby bud rises only as high as her knees. There are many movements that she can do on this level using torso, head, and arms and perhaps, leaning at times on her hand to support her body while she extends her legs and arms in various ways.

As the sun moves around the flowers, they bend their arms and throw their heads back as if they are drinking in the sun's rays. Similarly, when the rain comes down around them, they show that they are taking in the moisture. The baby bud reaches out in long stretches, first to the sun, then to the rain, and they hold out their arms to her as if trying to reach her.

When the flowers talk among themselves and laugh at the baby bud, they bend and sway and turn in place. The Children should move here and there all over the stage, creating interesting space patterns as they "search" before finding flowers to pick. The picked flowers scamper along behind the children (they are not carried). The children lead the flowers once around the stage and then leave them in a bunch while they play games (tossing balls, jump roping, and so forth). The flowers should slowly droop lower and lower until they are lying on the floor.

When the children return, they show surprise, a little sadness, and then shrug and leave. Elizabeth stays and dances sadly around the wilted flowers. She goes back to the garden by the route she took away from it (this could be two circles around the room) and searches from corner to corner before finding the baby bud. She takes it (leads it) a full circle or so around the room and finally places it in a crouching position in the center.

First the sun enters and then the rain. They move around the baby bud as if helping her to grow, then leave. Alone on the stage, the baby bud grows tall, showing her color with lifted head and turns and open arms. Elizabeth stays near the flower while her mother moves on the other side of the stage in pantomime.

The sun and the rain enter again, and everyone looks up at the flower who stands high and glorious—a winner at last.

The Pencil Party (ages 6–10)

Characters:

Ms. Forbes
School Custodian
Pencils, including No. 2's, red, other colored pencils, and
    more
Magic Markers (felt tipped) choose how many
Crayons, choose how many

The Pencil Party

School was over for the day. Ms. Forbes tidied up her desk and put her papers away. She checked her pencils which were neatly stacked and ready for use the next day. Then, she put on her coat and hat, took a last look about the room to make sure there was nothing she had forgotten and left the building.

A moment after she had gone, one of the Pencils jumped out of the container and announced to the others, "I'm darn tired of being pushed around all day by those children. I want to have some fun." So saying, he reached up and poked down a flurry of papers from a shelf. He began at once a long, wide scribble over one of the sheets. Here, there, and everywhere he went, making whatever marks came to his fancy.

"Stop! Stop it, I say!" called another Pencil. "You can't do that! You're not supposed to go around by yourself like that!" She jumped down and tried to erase everything the pencil had scribbled. Around and around she went after the pencil marks, trying to make them disappear.

"Oh, let him have his fun," the Other Pencils called. "It's a good idea."

"You know what?" the Magic Marker said darkly, "I'm going to make some thick black lines. The teacher never picks on me to do that in the class. Always in too much of a hurry, and she writes too fast." The Magic Marker moved slowly and powerfully along a piece of paper that had fallen on the floor near him. "This is fun," he called. "C'mon down you guys!"

"Yeah, I'd like to practice my cursive writing," said a Number 2 Pencil. "Us, too," called out some other Number 2's as they jumped down onto one of the scattered papers and began curving in and out, forming the letters Ms. Forbes had written on the blackboard.

"Well, I'm not going to practice anything!" said the Red Pencil. "I'm tired of marking papers with a check or a letter all day. I'm going to zigzag any way I darn please."

"Wait for us!" called 3 colored Pencils sliding out of their box. The Pencils together sharply zigzagged over several sheets of paper. They mixed red, blue, yellow, and green lines like a patchwork quilt.

"Hey, you all look like you're having so much fun. I'm gonna join you," cried a slender pink pencil as she unzipped herself from a pencil case. Off she went then, swirling around the paper and leaving fancy waves and curls behind her.

"Here we come, ready or not!" shouted the heavy Crayons.

"We're making capital letters." The thick wax Crayons moved high and low along the papers, up and down, making tall straight capital letters with wide, open curves.

"We should have done this long ago!" a Pencil roared "Boy! I really feel sharp today!"

The Pencils were having a wonderful time! All of a sudden, Ms. Forbes' sharp Red pencil stopped and listened. "Someone's coming!" the Pencil shouted. "Quick, get back in the box!"

All the Pencils jumped back to their places just in time. The door opened, and in walked the school Custodian. "Gads! What a mess!" he cried when he saw the papers all over the floor. He began stuffing them in the trash basket. Then he swept the floor of all the scraps. "The kids in Ms. Forbes class sure went wild today," he mumbled, shaking his head as he swept.

Suggestions

The pencils sit, crouch, and stand at different heights in the rear part of the room, facing front. Ms. Forbes uses the whole stage in getting ready to leave. She exaggerates the motions of putting on her hat and coat.

The kind of lines to be drawn by the pencils should be discussed and then explored in movement by the children. The manner of writing and choice of implements can be chosen according to the children's interests, although they will need suggestions to understand the range of possibilities. Other lines that can make interesting spatial patterns are letters of the alphabet, letters of individual children's names, script writing, punctuation marks, numbers, Roman numerals, calligraphy styles, and doodles.

The New Old Woman in the Shoe (ages 7–11)

Characters:

Reader
Child listening
Children who live in the shoe
Old woman

The New Old Woman in the Shoe

(Reader and child are seated to one side of the stage in front of a closed curtain—if there *is* a stage and a curtain.)

Reader: There was an old woman who lived in a shoe,
            She had too many kids to know what to do.
Child: Oh jeepers, I've heard this story before!
Reader: Be quiet and listen, there's more in store.
            (Curtain opens if there is one. Children enter from both sides, playing in ways the poem suggests.)
Reader: Here are her children, busy at play,
            jumping rope, skipping, enjoying the day
            When from the shoe comes a terrible shout
            And they turn to see the old woman come out.
            Waving the towel she holds in her hand,
            She shouts "You're all covered with mud and sand!
            Every one of you grimey as you can be,
            From the back of yer elbow to the front of yer knee!"
            At that the old woman scrubs them, I say,
            So hard, she very near scrubs them away!
            Then after a supper of milk and bread,
            She sends them trembling off to bed.

(The children, led by the old woman, march around the stage in a wide circle and lie down sleepily toward the rear, allowing room for the old woman to dance between and behind them.)

Reader: The children are sleeping, there is no sound,
Now the old woman tiptoes around,
To tuck them in tight and cover their toes,
And kiss each one on the tip of the nose.
Softly she sighs when at last she is through,
"What a good lot o' children I've got in my shoe!"
Child: She isn't as mean as the story books say,
Reader: No, it's just that she works so hard every day!
But now it is late, her day's work is done,
She looks at her children . . . and loves every one!
The tired old woman goes off to bed too,
Now you can't hear a whisper inside of the shoe.

(Curtain closes if there is one. Backstage, the children may put on or carry some symbol of the dream they are going to interpret.)

Reader: Here, the strange part of my story begins . . .
Child: About goblins and gremlins—or princes and kings,
Or outer space creatures with webbed feet and wings,
Or witches, and ghosts and mysterious things???
Reader: Shh! Listen and watch, I don't know what it means,
But children asleep fill their sleeping with dreams,
Just as the stars and moon fill the night,
Bringing to darkness moments of light.

(Curtain, if there is one, opens. Children are *lying* on stage as they were before. One at a time, they slowly rise and interpret their dream and then drift back to their original positions. Names of the children and what they dream will depend on the children in the class. Each child can decide on a subject and create an original verse for it. Two or three children may also interpret each dream.)

Reader: Beth is the first to dream tonight,

She dreams of a beautiful bird in flight.
Kay dreams of a dancer. How lightly she goes.
The stage is her dream world, the music, her toes.
Gregory dreams of a puppy dog pet,
Chasing a tail that it just can't get!
Sandra's a poet, her thoughts are clear
As she writes of her sorrow, her hope, her fear.
Jim is a driver, fast on the road,
With a ten-ton truck and a heavy load.
John is a scientist working in labs,
Doing his research on crayfish and crabs.
Laurie's a doctor—a pediatrician,
And her hobby is studying nuclear fission.
Now all of the beautiful dreams are through.

Child: Except the old woman's. Will she dream too?
(Old woman slowly rises and begins to move.)

Reader: Why, yes, I think that tonight she dreams,
Her apron's a costume that glitters and gleams.
How lovely she is. She has gone to a ball,
In silver shoes and a golden shawl.
She is dancing and happy when to her surprise,
She misses her children, and tears fill her eyes.
(Children rise. They greet the old woman and surround her.)

Reader: But then she looks up, and who does she see?
Why all of her darlings, as plain as can be!
Then she and her children dance all night long,
Like nine happy notes of a nightingale's song!

(Curtain, if there is one, closes while everyone continues dancing with high happy movements.)

Suggestions

All of the action is indicated in the poem. When the old woman scrubs the children their knees shake with fear as she grabs one or two and pretends to scrub them. The poem is read slowly at times to allow for movement, for example, when the children play in the beginning and when the old woman tiptoes around to tuck the children in. Music should be used throughout. Prokofiev's piano music makes fine accompaniment.

This creative movement play is especially suitable for presentation to a live audience.

Bibliography

Related Brain Research

Barrett, Lisa F.; *71/2 Lessons About the Brain*, Boston: Houghton Mifflin Harcourt, 2020.

CDC (Center for Disease Control) the National Youth Risk Behavior Study (YRBS), 2003. https://www.cdc.gov/healthyyouth/data/yrbs/files/2003/pdf/yrbs_2003_national_user_guide.pdf

Claxton, Guy; *Intelligence in the Flesh*, New Haven and London: Yale University Press, 2015.

Cloer, Daniel; Vision Magazine, June 2004, https://www.vision.org/.

Davis, Joel; *Mapping the Mind: Mapping the Mind: The Secrets of the Human Brain and How It Works*, Secaucus, NJ: Carol Publishing Co., 1997.

DeBord, Karen (Jan. 13, 1998), www.nncc.org/Child.Dev/brain-nc.html.

Demers, Stephen; *Mind, Brain, Health & Education*, 2010, www.mbhe.org/movement.

Dowd, Irene; *Teacher's Wisdom*, Dance Magazine, 2005.

Dowling, John E.; *Creating Mind*, New York and London: W.W. Norton, 1998.

Dwyer, Terence, James F. Sallis, Leigh Blizzard, Ross Lazarus, and Kimberlie Dean; *Relation of Academic Performance to Physical Activity and Fitness in Children* in Pediatric Exercise Science DOI: https://doi.org/10.1123/pes.13.3.225 In Print: Volume 13: Issue 3 Page Range: 225–237 *Pediatric Exercise Science*, 13(3):225–237, August 2001.

Etnier, J.L., W. Salazar, D.M. Landers, S.J. Petruzzello, M. Han, and P. Nowell; *The Influence of Physical Fitness and Exercise Upon Cognitive Functioning: A Meta-Analysis*, Psychology, Brain Research Reviews 2006.

Goetz, Magdalena Zernicka; *The Dance of Life*, New York: Basic Books, 2020.

Hamblin, J.M.D.; *If Our Bodies Could Talk*, New York: Doubleday, 2016.

Hawkins, Jeff, and Sandra Blakeslee; *On Intelligence, Times Books*, New York: Henry Holt and Co., 2004.

Hoffman, Donald D.; *Visual Intelligence: How We Create What We See*, New York and London: W.W. Norton, 1998.

Jenson, Eric; *Teaching with the Brain in Mind*, 2nd edition, ASCD, 2800 Shirlington Rd. Suite 1001, Arlington, VA 22206. 2005.

Jenson, Eric, and Liesl McConchie; *Brain-Based Learning: Teaching the Way Students Really Learn*, 3rd edition, Thousand Oaks: Corwin Press, Sage Publications, 2020.

Johnson, Steven; *Mind Wide Open: Your Brain and the Neuroscience of Everyday Life*, New York: Scribner, 2004.

Kotulak, Ronald; *Inside the Brain: Revolutionary Discoveries of How the Mind Works*, Kansas City, MO: Andrews McMeel Publishing Co., 1996 (pgs. xiv, xv, 5, 6, 7, 34–45).

Lovatt, Peter; *The Dance Cure*, New York: Harper Collins, 2021.

Medina, John; *Brain Rules: 12 Rules for Surviving at Home, Work and School*, 2008. Pear Press: https://www.pearpress.com/, 2nd edition updated and expanded, Seattle: Pear Press, 2014, www.brainrules.com.

Mitchell, Debby; *Learning Through Movement and Music* by GeoMotion Group Assembled by Jean Blaydes, www.humankinetics.com/products/all-products/Learning-Through-Movement-and-Music, 2012.

Nash, J. Madeleine; *Fertile Minds*: Sunday, June 24, 2001. http://content.time.com/time/magazine/article/0,9171,137214,00.html.

The National Dance Education Organization, www.ndeo.org/.

Peck, Judith; *Smart Starts in the Arts: Fostering Intelligence, Creativity and Serenity in the Early Years*. Mahwah: Imagination-Arts Publications, 2003.

Perry, Bruce; *The CIVITAS Healing Arts Project*, Duggal Visual Solutions, Feb. 11, 2015. https://duggal.com /contact. Corporate Offices Brooklyn Navy Yard, 63 Flushing Avenue, Building 25, Brooklyn NY 11205 brooklyn@duggal.com

Poser, Michael I., and Brenda Patoine *How Arts Training Improves Attention and Cognition*. Cerebrum, 2-4. (Sept. 2009).

Ramsburg, Dawn; Brain Development in Young Children, *Parent News*, April 1997.

Ratey, J.M.D.; *A User's Guide to the Brain*, New York: Pantheon, 2001.

Ratey, J.M.D.; *Spark: The Revolutionary New Science of Exercise and the Brain*, Boston: Little, Brown and Company, 2008.

Sousa, David A.; *How the Brain Learns*, 5th edition, Thousand Oaks: Corwin Press, 2016.

Sylwester, Robert; *Art for the Brain's Sake*, Educational Leadership, v56 n3 p31-35 Nov 1998

Thirteen WNET; *The Secret Life of the Brain*, New York, 2001. Distributed by PBS Home Video, www.pbs.org.

Van der Kolk, Bessel M.D.; *The Body Keeps the Score*, New York: Viking 2014.

Resources

Creative Movement

Barlin, Anne Lief, and Paul Barlin; *The Art of Learning Through Movement*, Los Angeles: Ward Ritchie Press, 1971.

Boorman, Joyce; *Creative Dance in the First Three Grades*, New York: David McKay, Co., 1969.

Cratty, Briant J.; *Active Learning*, Englewood Cliffs, NJ: Prentice-Hall, 1971.

Dimondstein, Geraldine; *Children Dance in the Classroom*, New York: Macmillan Co., 1971.

Hawkins, Alma; *Creating Through Dance*, 2nd edition, Princeton: Princeton Book Co., 1987.

H'Doubler, Margaret N.; *Dance, a Creative Art Experience*, Paperback, Madison: University of Wisconsin Press, 2003.

Murray, Ruth Lovell; *Dance in Elementary Education*, 3rd edition, New York: Harper & Row, 1975.

North, Marion; *Body Movement for Children*, Boston: Plays, 1972.

Peck, Judith; *Leap to the Sun: Learning through Dynamic Play*, Prentice-Hall 1979, available: https://iapbooks.com.

Russell, Joan; *Creative Dance in the Primary School*, 3rd edition, Paperback, London: Northcote House, 1987.

Tanner Dance Program, an Improvisational Dance Program and Resource Based on Virginia Tanner's Teaching. University of Utah, 1721 Campus Center Drive, Salt Lake City, UT 84112 801-581-7374 tannerdance@utah.edu.

Wiener, Jack, and John Lidstone; *Creative Movement for Children*, New York: Van Nostrand Reinhold, 1969.

230 Bibliography

Resources

Musical Accompaniment

Bela Bartok, *For Children, vols. 1 and 2 Bela Bartok*, www.ccmusic.com/search?q=bela+bartok&mod=AC Also on Amazon: https://www.amazon.com

Cawthray, Chris; *Move—Music for Creative Movement + Modern Dance*, 2001, https://dance-teacher.com/music-for-creativemovement/ Also on Amazon: https://www.amazon.com/

Chappelle, Eric; *Music for Creative Dance: Contrast and Continuum*, vol.1,1993,https://music.apple.com/us/album/music-forcreative-dance-contrast-and-continuum-vol-1/661453067 Also on Amazon: https://www.amazon.com/

Claude Debussy *Children's Corner (Jeux D'enfants)*, www.ccmusic.com/search?q=debussy&mod=AC. www.kimboed.com/.

Feierabend, John M.; *Music for Creative Movement*, www.giamusic.com/store/resource/music-for-creative-movement-3-cd-set-recordingcd903 Also on Amazon: https://www.amazon.com/

Kimbo Educational Records; Music & Movement for Children. https://www.kimboed.com Choose Dance Catalog, ballet, Customer Service 800.631.2187

Sergei Prokofieff: Piano Music Varied Rhythms and Songs. Listening on line is a treat https://classicalmusiconly.com/composer/sergei-prokofiev/works/tv

Index

Page locators in *italics* indicate a figure.